LIVE LIFE AGGRESSIVELY!

What Self Help Gurus Should Be Telling You

MIKE MAHLER

Live Life Aggressively!

A Mahler's Aggressive Strength LLC Book/May 2011

Cover photo courtesy of Ayame Hollings
www.orangekettlebellclub.com

Back cover courtesy of David Griffin
www.davidgriffinphotography.com

Front and back cover design work by Kyle Provost

Editing by Teresa Blazy and Alex Goetzfried

Final editing and proofreading by Sarina Derksen

ISBN 978-0-578-08475-6

This book is dedicated to my good friend Jim Tirey as well as the great men and women that serve and have served in the United States Armed Forces. Thanks for everything you do for us.

Jim was a constant source of support when I first decided to pursue a career in fitness. Jim also served in the military for most of his life and represents everything that is great about the wonderful men and women that serve in the armed forces. Jim passed away a few years ago and his presence is missed but will never be forgotten.

This book is also dedicated to everyone that has improved the life of another being.

FOREWORD
By Steve Cotter

Don't be fooled by the title. Live Life Aggressively! What Self-help Gurus Should Be Telling You by Mike Mahler is not a book advocating violence or aggression toward people. Rather it is a call-to-action, an invitation for you, the reader to stand up and take account of your own life and your actions.

This book is not group hug. It is more like a bucket of ice-cold water tossed on you while you slumber in your warm, comfy habits.

There is a saying that "the truth hurts" and unlike the self-help gurus which proliferate the talk shows and books shelves, Mahler challenges you to take an honest look at yourself, at your strengths and weaknesses, your successes and failures, and reminds you that if you do the hard work of self-reflection, you will come out happier and more fulfilled, because you will see yourself as you really are, warts and all. Armed with this self-realization, you can begin your journey in earnest, to a more fulfilling and actualized state of being.

In his tell-it-like-it-is style of communicating, Mahler lays out a brutally transparent formula for success and contentment. Rather than fill you with grandiose affirmations and feel-good self-dialogue, he strips off the gloves and tells you WHY you are losing the good fight by lying to yourself about who your really are. You may not realize it, but Mahler is your friend, and Live Life Aggressively is the heart-to-heart dialogue that all but your true friends are unable and unwilling to give you.

Precisely because the author does not try to be your buddy, and because he is not influenced by if you like him or not, he can speak straight to you and in this over-hyped, over-promised and under-delivered media-driven environment we live in, straight talk is a rare commodity indeed.

As an industry leader in my profession, I travel all around the world and have met many if not most of the industry "gurus" hawking their methods and philosophies. The majority of these salesmen do not practice what they preach. I get asked to endorse products and programs all the time. More and more I say thanks but no thanks, because I know that a lot of the things being sold are rehashed garbage. When Mike Mahler invited me to write a forward for this book, I said "of course". The reason is because the man does what he says he is going to do, he practices what he preaches and he leads from the front. I respect the man and there is a reason why he commands sold-out audiences wherever he lectures. What he shares with you in this book is what he has learned through living - no gimmicks, no fluff, and no empty promises. Just straight talk from a straight man, literally and figuratively.

Whether you are a pacifist or a hawk, a carnivore or a vegan, a scholar or a warrior - as you read through this exceptional book of wisdom you will appreciate the importance of taking charge of your life and Live Life Aggressively!

— *Steve Cotter, Founder and Director of IKFF,*
International Kettlebell and Fitness Federation, www.ikff.com

CONTENTS

INTRODUCTION
by Ken Blackburn

Many of the self-help books on the market are not helpful at all. If anything, they offer the reader a temporary emotional buzz but fall short when it comes to true-life application. In this sense, they have the potential to be self-destructive. Readers repeatedly purchase book after book with no desired change and they eventually lose hope.

Thus, it's important to clarify this book is NOT that. This book was not written with the goal making you feel warm and fuzzy. Actually, much of what Mike proposes may initially make you feel worse via taking you out of your comfort zone. True change is not a passive process and requires a brutal self inventory as a catalyst for moving forward and achieving what you want in life.

Mike's focus is to induce real/lasting change and that comes as result of being aggressively honest with yourself, using pressure to your advantage, running toward risk rather than away from it and having a clear vision of what you want and what you are willing to sacrifice to get it. His plan may not be easy, but it works.

In addition, Mike is an excellent role model for everything he preaches. His philosophies are based on both his successes and his struggles. The openness in which he shares his life experiences is congruent with the theme of honesty and courage that permeates the book. Mike is one of the best examples I know of yin/yang as it relates to being a balanced person. Although he may be in your face at times, he is also one of the most generous and compassionate people you will ever meet. He will speak with intense passion about a number of topics, but also couple it with humor. His words can be harsh, but he empathizes with the figurative and literal fights we all face.

As many of us watched Mike's fitness career develop over the years, it was no surprise that he morphed into the strength & conditioning icon he is today. Throughout his journey, Mike shared his ideas on fitness, nutrition, wellness and overall life success via numerous articles, his website etc. So, with his prolific writing talents, it came as no surprise that he chose to author this book.

I've been fortunate enough to have Mike as a mentor and friend over the years. He shared many of the philosophies and strategies in this book and they played a huge role in my success. You will enjoy the read and significantly benefit from it if you are willing to commit to what he outlines. As he will mention later in the book, true success and happiness come to those who "save nothing for the swim back".

IT IS TIME TO
LIVE LIFE AGGRESSIVELY

The word aggressive gets a bad rap and there is constant pressure on people, especially men, to be less aggressive. In fact, the male hormone testosterone is often associated with violence, when in reality men with optimal testosterone levels are anything but violent. According to top strength coach Charles Poliquin, it is men with low testosterone that are often violent as they try to over compensate for having low testosterone. Moreover, let me remind you that it is old men in offices that start wars, and old men are not known for having high testosterone. Ironically they start the wars, and then send young men with high testosterone to fight the battles.

While aggressive can mean violent, it also means to move forward with strong intent or purpose. That is what this book is all about. This book is a slap in the face!

It will force you out of your comfort zone, and will help you remember what you need to know to move forward with purpose. It is about taking charge of your life, and striving for greatness, rather than accepting mediocrity, or a life of quiet desperation. That is what it means to live life aggressively! It means to live with strong purpose and resolve. This book covers areas that few have the courage to talk about, and that is the problem. It is the white elephant in the room that everyone wants to ignore. Instead of confronting this problem, most people waste time watching nonsense like American Idol and Glee.

Most, if not all self-help books are overly complicated compilations of nonsense, which fail to offer anything that you can use to improve your life.

Will saying daily affirmations help you improve your life? Probably not.

Will faking it till you make it help you get to the Promised Land? Lets ask the ladies, how many of you actually enjoy faking it? Don't raise your hands all at once.

Will books that encourage men to act like women, and women to act like men, really help either sex? Absolutely not, and the current wussification of America is all too evident of that.

Will books that tell you to write down your five, ten, or twenty girly goals really help you? No, because they distract you from being fully present in the moment and this moment is all you have.

The past is dead, and the future is not here. As if we don't have enough to worry about now, we have to worry about where we will be in the future as well. Americans worry too much as it is. Being fully in the moment is the best thing you can do for a bright future. No one knows what the future has in store.

As the saying goes, want to make God laugh? Tell God your plans.

Self help books are so focused on making you feel good about yourself, that they fail to help you be honest with yourself.

Without brutal honesty you will never move forward. Without a strong sense of purpose, and passion, you will never persevere through the inevitable plethora of hard times that are coming your way in life.

It is time to get real and cut out all the fluff. Decide what you want to do in life, put together a plan of action, and execute that plan. If the first plan does not work, come up with another plan. If that one fails go back to the drawing board and come up with yet another plan. If that one fails, well you get the idea.

If it is important to you, and something you genuinely want, not something others think you should have, you will make the necessary sacrifices. Want to know something crazy? You will actually enjoy the process. People that do what they love work harder than anyone else, and they love the hard work.

Forget about vacations! Who needs a vacation from the thrill of waking up and doing what you love everyday? Nothing takes the place of doing what excites you for a career. No relationship can take its place. No material gain comes close. Accolades from others cannot compare. Those of you that are already doing what you love know exactly what I am talking about. Those of you that are not there, have no clue what you are missing out on.

Life does not have to be drudgery with a few happy moments. Life does not have to be boring to the point where you have to drown your miseries with drugs and alcohol every weekend. You do not have to settle for just getting by. You can strive for greatness. It is the striving that is the juice, not the achievement. This is something many fail to realize, even though every spiritual practice discusses it.

As important as following your bliss is, it is not the only thing that matters. Real success comes from knowing yourself and what you are capable of. True happiness comes from taking the time to do the necessary self-inventory to evolve. Perfection is not possible yet in some ways there is something all too perfect about imperfections.

This book is not about how to get rich and make millions. I am not a millionaire nor do I care to be one. Not to say there is anything wrong with being a millionaire. Sure I love making money and having a great income. Making lots of money is fine if that is your goal. However, I think you will find that being attached to goals makes it impossible to really be happy, and that is what real success is all about. It is not about keeping up with the Joneses, expensive vacations, or acquiring material things that you don't need or genuinely want. It is about being free to live your life and to not be at the mercy of circumstances. It is about waking up every day and enjoying a career that makes you excited, and empowers you and others.

It is about not being a chump in life and taking charge. Not waiting for others to tell you what to do but deciding for yourself what makes you happy and having the courage to pursue it, even when it seems that all the odds are stacked against you.

I am not here to motivate you. I am here to make you think. That is what this book is all about: provoking thought! Will you agree with everything I have to say? I hope not, because if you do then only one of us is thinking, and trust me I think all the time! I do not want to be a guru, or someone that you come to for advice. I am not a life coach or a motivational speaker, and have no desire to become one. I do not have all the answers and have never claimed to. However, I do know what it is like to be miserable, and living without passion. I also know exactly what it is like to be genuinely happy, and fully present in the moment. Trust me on this one, if you do not remember anything else in this book remember this: it is much better to follow your passion and work harder than you have ever worked in your life, then to sit back in a cushy job and be a minimalist for the rest of your life.

Embrace the struggle, the person you will become in the process is worth the necessary suffering. The struggle is where you know yourself fully!

This book is essentially a compilation of many articles I have written over the years. Many of the chapters were articles in my online magazine. Others have never been revealed until now.

I find that the best books these days are compilations of many articles. For example top strength coach Pavel Tsatsouline's best book in my opinion is Beyond Bodybuilding, which is a compilation of articles that he wrote for a variety of fitness magazines. Another excellent example is Randall Strossen's Ironmind: Stronger Minds, Stronger Bodies. When people write books they tend to include way too much filler and not enough real information. They fail to get to the point, and waste a lot of time. Lets face it, time is in short supply these days so we need to be careful with it. With articles, writers tend to get to the point, and I have always found I learn more from articles than books these days. This book is fluff free and fairly concise at just over one hundred and fifty pages. It is meant to be accessible, and not something that occupies too much of your valuable time. I realize that you only want to spend so much time away from Facebook, texting, and having high quality conversations at coffee shops.

Some of the chapters are long and others are brief and that is on purpose. This is not a book that you have to read from start to finish. Pick a section or chapter that catches your interest and start there. Each chapter covers a theme so you can easily read one chapter a day for a metaphorical kick in the ass when needed.

There are three main categories to this book:
1. Section one covers what self-help gurus should be telling you.
2. Section two is my favorite section and covers the importance of taking self inventory, and being brutally honest with yourself and others.
3. Section three covers my thoughts on success and happiness.

There are very few unique ideas in this book if any. Much of it is common sense that has been forgotten, while other ideas are things that I have learned from studying all the great religions and philosophies in college, and through my many life experiences. Everything that one needs to know about how to succeed, and evolve in life has been said, and definitely has been articulated better than me. That being said, it can never be emphasized enough, and the more you see, hear, and feel it, the better.

Mahatma Gandhi once said that, "Whatever you do in life will be insignificant, but it is very important that you do it."

If one of the greatest men of all time thinks what he did to revolutionize a country is insignificant, you can imagine where you and I fall on the spectrum of importance. This is something to remember when we live our lives consumed by our illusions of grandeur.

Regardless, we all have a duty and getting my story to you is part of my duty.

What you choose to do with it is your duty.

SECTION ONE:
WHAT SELF-HELP GURUS SHOULD BE TELLING YOU

WHY YOU MUST
OPTIMIZE YOUR HORMONES

Self-help gurus never talk about the importance of having an optimal hormonal environment. Not only is this important for your physical and mental health, it is critical for having the drive to evolve as a person and have the energy and perseverance to pursue your goals. Forget about saying moronic affirmations to yourself, or faking it until you make it. Create an optimal hormone environment and you will have real confidence, real drive, and will not have to fake anything.

In my fitness business I do a lot of consulting with people to help them with their health and fitness. I spend a lot of time looking at people's hormone levels, which provides critical information to help them achieve their goals. I can tell a lot about how someone is feeling by looking at his or her hormone levels. For example if a man has very high levels of estrogen and SHBG (sex hormone binding globulin) then it is a certainty that his sex drive is very low, and that his drive for life in general is low, because both are connected. An optimal testosterone to estrogen ratio is critical for a man to feel at his best. Forget about having a good mood and being a driven person with poor access to testosterone. Another example is women with poor progesterone to estrogen ratios. Women need progesterone to keep estrogen in balance. When progesterone is too low women develop estrogen dominance, which causes a lot of fat to be gained on the glutes and legs. Moreover, a woman's mood will be in the toilet without adequate progesterone levels.

I say it often at my courses; at the end of the day we are our hormones. If our hormones are optimal we will wake up feeling great, ready to take on the world. If they are not optimal, we won't even want to get out of bed to face the day. We will have to force ourselves out, and drink tons of coffee to get going, and keep going. Sound familiar?

I began my investigation into hormonal balancing in 2003 for personal reasons. I'm now 37 years old with the hormonal profile of a healthy eighteen-year-old. My mood is upbeat; my experience of life intense, my training gains are solid and my sex drive is optimal. I'm not boasting, I tell you this because what I learned and recommend works. It works for me and will work for you as well. It took many years of private research and testing to get where I am now, but not too long ago things were much different for me.

Back in 2000 I experienced many of the signs and symptoms of andropause, i.e., my sex drive was low; my mood was poor; my zeal for life was so non-existent that I was (allegedly) spotted watching a Sex in the City marathon - just kidding! Fortunately, my estrogen levels have never been that high! Both undesirable and avoidable - andropause is all the same considered normal for men in their fifties but in my case, I was only twenty-eight! Unfortunately, I was far from alone: I have many chronologically young male and female clients whose hormone levels would be unhealthy for men and women in their fifties. Epidemiological, this problem is becoming more widespread for reasons beyond the scope of this chapter. Suffice to say that the primary reasons are poor diet, environmental toxicity, and also societal pressure. Being a man is no longer celebrated and neither is being a real woman for that matter. Both men and women are confused on how to be true to their respective sex and as we can see all too clearly the consequences are disastrous.

Eventually, I got tired of being tired, and decided to take charge of my health and my life. It was a frustrating start as I realized how few health professionals genuinely understood hormone optimization. The advice I received was generally trivial and in some cases irrational and dangerous. Most "experts" offered to sugar coat my symptoms rather than determine any root causes. The more I talked to these "experts" the more I realized I needed to resolve this problem on my own.

One essential factor in optimizing hormones is your ability to handle stress. The ability to handle stress and the ability to experience happiness are one and the same. Studies indicate that people with a naturally high stress threshold, also display an inherent predisposition for happiness. Denying stress and running on adrenaline (which is what I'd been doing) will only get you so far. Eventually, you'll crash, and when you crash, you'll burn. Make no mistake, the stress hormone, cortisol, must be within reasonable range to optimize your hormones and thus feel great. Keep this in mind - too little cortisol is just as bad if not worse than too much cortisol. Humans require stress to thrive and reach our full potential; however, too much stress, and its attendant hormone, cortisol, will degrade us...and there are no exceptions to this rule. Too much cortisol cannibalizes the sex hormones, such as pregnenolone, and in turn DHEA, androstenedione, and finally, testosterone.

People tend to focus on testosterone or estrogen when addressing hormone optimization. Yes both are important but both are downstream hormones. To best optimize hormone levels is to focus on the big picture and the hormones that have the most power. There are three such hormones: leptin, insulin, and adrenaline. Of these three, leptin is the most important. Insufficient leptin further compromises testosterone and growth hormone. I learned about the importance of Leptin in Byron Richard's excellent book Mastering Leptin.

What exactly is leptin? A hormone produced by fat cells, leptin was discovered in 1994. Leptin's primary job is restoring fat reserves when energy (food) is consumed. This is a biological survival mechanism to increase survival chances in case of famine. (These days however, the closest most people we know approach famine is their two-hour downtime between meals!) After restoring fat reserves, leptin determines how much energy the body needs and where it's best spent. Leptin, in fact, leads the entire hormonal cascade.

When leptin levels drop, the brain receives a signal (from another hormone, grehlin) that it's time to eat. Ideally you'll pick healthy options, e.g. high-quality foods to replenish the brain's neurotransmitters and refill liver and muscle glycogen.

When you eat a meal, leptin levels rise again, signaling the brain that enough calories have been consumed and it's time to stop eating. Insulin levels also rise with food intake and insulin's job is to get as much nutrition as possible into the liver and muscles. If the muscles and liver are already full of nutrients, then nutrient spillover occurs and excess calories are stored as fat. When leptin is working properly it prevents nutrient spillover by telling insulin to shut off after your tank is full.

When you don't eat enough calories (or more precisely, don't derive enough energy from the food you eat) for too long a time, leptin signals the thyroid hormones to decrease metabolic rate in order to conserve energy. In addition to slowing down fat loss, a sluggish metabolic rate will hamper sex hormone production and anabolism in general. Since the production of sex hormones is energy intensive, if the body isn't receiving adequate fuel, all stores will go to maintenance and repair before growth. Growth means muscle tissue, among other things, and muscle maintenance and growth are your best tools for fat loss and optimal body composition. Without adequate sex hormone production, in particular testosterone and growth hormone, you will not be able to build muscle. The best you can hope for is skinny fat, and taking up less space on the planet does not equate to lean and healthy. Skinny fat is still poor body composition.

Neither are high levels of leptin the same as optimal levels. Ironically, overweight people have high leptin levels, but the brain doesn't "know" those levels are high due to a condition called leptin resistance, wherein the satiety messages issued from leptin never make it to the brain's receptors, which generally results in excess calorie intake before satiety is registered. Overeating in general, obviously results in excess calories being stored as fat.

Hard training athletes can get away with an unseemly high calorie intake, since their energy demand is higher than the average person. Their insulin sensitivity is high, and their muscles store and metabolize more glycogen. The average person's insulin liver and muscle glycogen storage is considerably more limited and further, their insulin resistance may be compromised. Once the average person's liver and muscle glycogen stores are refilled, (if they were ever depleted in the first place) the rest of the meal's energy value goes to fat storage, to be used - ideally - another day. This is why I think post-workout, high-carbohydrate "recovery" shakes are a mistake, at least for the average person of sub-optimal body composition (ie, too fat) who consume adequate amounts of carbohydrates throughout the day already. Combined with less-than-optimal insulin sensitivity in the muscles, it's a recipe for increasing body fat.

Excessive calorie intake is the fast track to leptin resistance. Since it's hard to eat excess of the so-called "clean" foods, excess calories usually come from junk foods. For most people, frequent intake of fast foods and other junk foods brings them to a bad end: leptin resistance.

Every time you eat food in excess (of energy required by the body) leptin and insulin levels surge. The larger and more calorie dense the meal, the higher the surge and the longer the duration. You know the rap: the excess stimulation causes the cellular receptors to develop resistance to the continual flood of hormones. Once the receptors become resistant, they require more stimulation (food intake) to respond with a satiety signal. This condition, leptin resistance, is analogous to becoming a human fat storage organism. An ignoble accomplishment compared to the heights of real human potential.

Leptin resistance leads to insulin resistance, which further increases leptin resistance. With insulin resistance, you no longer have insulin sensitivity. When you have insulin sensitivity, you only need to secrete a small amount of insulin to get calories into the muscle and liver. Your receptor uptake of insulin is strong and efficient. When you have insulin resistance, your receptors are weak and worn out. As a result you require a much higher insulin response from overeating to get calories into the muscles and liver. What ever is left over, which is a lot, will be stored as fat. High insulin also results in an inevitable blood sugar crash, which makes you hungry again. Thus you have an insatiable urge to eat and the entire process starts all over again. I will discuss insulin resistance shortly.

Leptin resistance is a serious health issue. Essentially you are over feeding your body but the perception from your brain is that you are starving. Thus, even though you're eating a lot, your metabolic rate will slow down just like someone who is undereating. A slowed down metabolic rate again slows down fat loss or brings it to a screeching halt. Moreover, a hampered metabolic rate puts the breaks on sex hormone production. The end result is you're fat, tired, and have no sex drive. You do not have energy to put in intense weight training workouts to build muscle and ramp up testosterone and growth hormone. Even if you do get the intense workouts in, you do not have the testosterone and growth hormone production to recover from arduous workouts.

Just like many things in life, you must create an optimal hormone balance that is right for you. This will vary with each person. Just like every hormone you do not want leptin too high or too low. You want just enough for optimal functioning. While there is a blood test that you can do for leptin it is really not necessary. If you are overweight you have leptin resistance.

The way to get out of leptin resistance is to give your body a break. Just like we need vacations from work, our receptors need a vacation from having to deal with large volumes of food delivered often. The first thing you need to do is make better food choices.

Eat a balance of protein, fat, and carbs at every meal. A good starting point is 30% protein, 40% carbs, and 30% fat popularized by Barry Sears as "The Zone" diet. This won't be the perfect ratio for everyone - you will have to experiment to see what works best for you but it is a reasonable starting point.

Trying to lose fat? Take a page from Byron Richard's book, stick to two to three meals a day, with five to eight hours between meals. The extended food-free meal breaks provide opportunities for the body to call on stored fat for energy. Instead of snacks, your body will fuel itself with free fatty acids, as long as you're not in the aerobic zone. To ensure a growth hormone surge while sleeping each night, best to quit eating at least four hours before bedtime. GH optimizes fat loss and muscle growth, which is all the more reason to prioritize the recommended 7-9 hours of good quality sleep each night. What could be more hard core than aggressive sleeping? And the longer the duration, and greater intensity the sleep, the better the results. So turn off GH killers, such as late night television and internet as well as alcohol, and apply yourself to better sleeping and recovery habits.

For hard training athletes - especially those with low body fat levels, three meals a day will probably not cut it. Four meals per day with about four hours between meals is better. Still, cut off eating three hours before bedtime for best recovery from tough workouts.

Nutrition supplements also have a place in optimizing leptin. One supplement that everyone can benefit from is magnesium. Magnesium is needed to extract energy from food and for optimal insulin function. The more energy you extract from food the less you have to eat to feel great. Magnesium's benefits go on forever.

Next, lets spend some time discussing another master control hormone: Insulin. Without adequate insulin, our cells literally starve and our bodies die. This is why type-1 diabetics must self-administer insulin injections. A type-1 diabetic is unable to generate insulin and must have an external source or die. On the other hand, too much insulin production (due to insulin resistance) leads to type-2 diabetes and cellular degeneration. Fortunately, type-2 diabetes can be both avoided and reversed with diet modification.

Insulin levels within the optimal range are balanced with the hormone glucagon. Protein provides the body what it needs to make glucagon, so a simple rule of thumb is to eat protein and carbs at every meal. (There's no need for precise ratios, just be sure to eat protein with every meal and you'll be fine.) Further, have a healthy fat with every meal. While fat has neither negative nor positive effect on insulin response, it's a critical component in overall hormone production and the body requires fats to produce the sex hormones, such as DHEA and testosterone. Long term low-fat dieting, not surprisingly, results in low levels of critical sex hormones.

At this point, you may wonder why insulin is the foundation of overall hormone optimization? I've explained the role it plays in maintaining life itself, and why it mustn't be too low, but let's see what happens when insulin is too high.

The reason people gain fat from high carbohydrate consumption is because of the insulin spike that follows any high carbohydrate meal. When you eat a significant amount of carbohydrates, (such as a bowl of pasta) your blood glucose levels go through the roof, requiring a compensatory surge of insulin to bring that glucose back down within normal range. Time after time, meal after meal, the consequence is poor body composition, e.g., excess body fat stores, poor mood and poorer health. Excess insulin production resulting from dietary carbohydrates increases body fat, which in turn compromises sex hormone manufacture and metabolism. The fatter you are, the more estrogen receptors you'll have, which reduces the cellular access to testosterone. This is why you can't utilize extra testosterone, no matter how much you are making (or supplementing) if insulin is not properly managed.

In short, insulin must be balanced with glucagon. Insulin drives nutrients into cells for storage, while glucagon mobilizes cellular energy stores to circulate in the blood stream on demand. High insulin levels block the release of glucagon, which, among other chores, is critical for brain function.

Excess insulin in the body indicates excess calories, in particular, carbohydrates. Worse, the more carbohydrates you eat, the more free radicals are produced in the digestive process, compromising the immune system. Overly high insulin levels also call on cortisol as a backup, which leads to excess cortisol production. Remember, excess cortisol destroys the desirable hormones: testosterone, DHEA, and human growth hormone. Adding cortisol into this game increases insulin resistance by indirectly increasing insulin production. This is because the pancreas pumps out more insulin to lower the cortisol. As if that weren't bad enough, prolonged excess cortisol eventually destroys the cortisol sensitive cells in the brain. This is why more and more research is linking Alzheimer's disease to lifelong excess cortisol.

Because of continual elevated cortisol production, the condition of insulin resistance results in decreased levels of other, beneficial, hormones. The master hormone, pregnenolone, opts between making DHEA, progesterone, or cortisol but when glucagon levels are inadequate the body must opt for survival rather than thriving. Consequently, pregnenolone does not go to DHEA and progesterone production, thus DHEA doesn't convert to androstenedione and our theoretical (at this point) androstenedione never converts to testosterone. This cascade of failure illustrates why trying to increase any single hormone before managing the play of insulin and glucagon is ineffective and a waste of your supplement budget.

The third critical hormone that must be optimized for overall health and to increase your drive for success is adrenaline. The main adrenaline hormones are norepinephrine and epinephrine. Both are catecholamines, secreted by the adrenals, which trigger the "fight or flight" response (also known as an adrenaline rush) providing an energy and strength boost by way of the central nervous system for 2-15 minutes. When facing a legitimate stressor, i.e. an emergency, we rely on these hormones to overcome and persevere. Epinephrine, also referred to as adrenaline, is what gets you out of bed in the morning; it further gives you an edge every time you take on a challenge. Adrenaline gives us energy for intense workouts and, in the form of norepinephrine, for the mental demands of life.

Most people in modern society have chronically jacked up adrenaline levels. Day-to-day living, taking a lot of stimulants, such as caffeine or ingredients in energy drinks, only increases the load on their already overworked adrenal glands. While epinephrine works in the body, increasing oxygen and glucose levels while suppressing digestive and immune systems, norepinephrine works similarly, but adds a bonus psychoactive element. Thus every time you take a stimulant such as coffee the message to the brain is a consciousness of stress.

Chronically elevated adrenaline always results in adrenaline resistance, a condition wherein the various adrenaline receptors become desensitized. In an adrenaline-sensitive system, adrenaline causes blood sugar to rise (to be burned for energy), while simultaneously releasing lipids into the blood stream (the fat-burning part), thus adrenaline can aid us in breaking down fat deposits for energy. Unfortunately, in an adrenaline-resistant system, since the receptors are dulled, the message is either delayed or worse, never gets through. Thus, the system stores instead of burning the available energy sources and, worse yet, tends to store the released lipids into already-existing stubborn fat deposits, like hips and thighs in women, and love handles and upper back fat in men. In addition to the increasing fat deposit stores, adrenaline resistance, allowed to run its course, ends with severe energy lows and general fatigue. Receptors worn out by chronic stimulation eventually shut down, leaving you lagging all day. Any zeal you once had for life is now vaporized like the Las Vegas job market.

Unfortunately, the effects of adrenaline resistance don't stop at increased fat storage and decreased energy levels. Chronically elevated adrenaline brings inflammation: every secretion of adrenaline triggers a complement of the stress hormone, cortisol, a counter-response to the system's inflammatory response to adrenaline. Like adrenaline, cortisol--in the appropriate doses is helpful. The problem, again, is too much of a good thing such as when cortisol levels are chronically elevated is not good. In an optimal scenario, cortisol is released to reduce the inevitable inflammation (by way of suppressing the immune response) triggered by adrenaline, and everything is as it should be thus homeostasis ensues. The problem arises when cortisol is chronically released in response to an adrenaline-resistant system - resulting is a continual feedback loop of stress hormones. Worse, unlike adrenaline, cortisol doesn't release fatty acids for energy, but goes the quick and dirty route of muscle catabolism. So you see, between the fatty acid storage and muscle catabolism, how adrenaline resistance (at least in the realm of optimal body composition) is truly a worst-case scenario.

Building and retaining muscle mass is critical to body leanness. If your goals include fat loss, you'll want to add muscle to improve your ratio of lean body mass to fat and building muscle is virtually impossible in the face of adrenaline resistance.

We need sufficient testosterone and growth hormone to feel our best and thrive. But the excess cortisol (from the excess adrenaline) pulls the plug on muscle gains on one front, by flat-lining production of the anabolic sex hormones. When your central nervous system is in continual survival mode, available energy is no longer delegated to anabolism (i.e. tissue growth and repair) but instead to survival mode (i.e. inflammation by suppressing the immune system.) Decreased sex hormone production is the kiss of death for muscle gains, fat loss, powerful immunity and a healthy zeal for life. You want to optimize your sex hormone levels and feel great? Here's the hitch: you must address adrenaline resistance.

Crush adrenaline resistance by sleeping more, meditating daily, and not relying on stimulants such as coffee and energy drinks. One or two cups of coffee is not a big deal and has benefits for the brain and insulin sensitivity. However, more than that causes problems for most and eventually leads to adrenaline resistance. Getting rid of toxins in the body is also important so you have more real energy to take charge of your life. Knowing this, it makes sense to eat a diet both clean and free of toxins. Consuming ample organic fruits and vegetables provides the liver antioxidants to counter the effects of toxins released from the fat cells. While the nutrition benefit per se of organic food over non-organic food is negligible at best, organic food has less surface toxins from sprays which ideally translates into a lower toxic load on the system, therefore less burden on the liver and finally, decreased stubborn body fat.

What happens when you clean up and lock in your diet, master stress levels and train hard with adequate recovery time? Well, in my case, when given the opportunity to optimize themselves, my hormones adjusted themselves into not only adequate, but ideal ranges.

In fact, my last saliva test showed my androstenedione, progesterone, DHEA, DHT and testosterone all in optimal ranges. I've achieved this through diet modification, proper sleep and restoration, hard training and a few key supplements, primarily Magnesium Oil, zinc citrate, and an incredible South African herb called Bulbine Natalensis. Bulbine has been shown in studies to increase testosterone by 300% and lower estrogen by 35%. It has also been shown to out perform Viagra as a sex enhancer. I am working on a testosterone optimizing supplement that will include Bulbine as well as some other outstanding ingredients to optimize testosterone.

The subject of hormone optimization is complex, but at its core it is addressed by optimizing the three big players: leptin, insulin, and adrenaline. This is something self-help gurus should be telling you, without an optimal hormone environment you will never be genuinely happy or have the fire to take charge of your life and make all your dreams come true. We have to act to optimize hormones, by taking charge of our life but we also have to have optimal hormones in order to take charge of our life and stay on the path long enough to achieve success. Do not let anyone tell you otherwise. Always look at the personal results of whoever is giving you advice. Does he or she have the personal example to back up what he or she is professing?

WHERE DO YOU GO FROM HERE?

Recommended Steps

- Take a saliva hormone test to see where your levels are. I have info on my site regarding this at www.mikemahler.com

- Have high quality protein, healthy fat, and low glycemic carbohydrates at every meal, including post-workout shakes. You'll have to experiment to determine what the ideal ratio is for you. A good place to start is 30% protein, 40% carbs, and 30% fat. You needn't perfect the ratios to benefit, just eat all three macronutrients with every meal.

- Take at least six hour stretches between each meal - no snacking.

- Get all food from organic real food sources.

- Get all carbohydrates from fruits and veggies.

- Keep coffee at 1-2 cups per day, or cut it out completely.

- Address emotional issues, such as childhood traumas. If you fail to do this, hormones will never balance. I discuss this in the chapter on embracing compassion or being destroyed by anger.

- Meditate twenty minutes daily. This is beneficial any time of day but has particular benefits after workouts and before bedtime. Daily practice of tai chi or chi-kung is also useful.

- Take charge of your life and the responsibility that comes with it.

- Incorporate intense cardio training, such as interval sprints, into your routine to ramp up growth hormone.

- Engage in heavy weight training with short breaks (60-80% of your one rep max with 60-second breaks). Focus on compound movements.

- Use Ancient Minerals Magnesium Oil before bedtime and take 30mg of zinc every morning. More info can be found on my website www.mikemahler.com

RECOMMENDED READING

Mastering Leptin By Byron Richards

- This is a great book on how to optimize leptin and other hormones.

The Anti-aging Zone, by Barry Sears Ph.D

- Solid info on diet and hormone levels; however, I don't agree with his conclusion that intense exercise is bad for you. Neither do I think you need to follow his 30-40-30 diet plan, nor eat five times per day.

The Anti-estrogenic Diet and Maximum Muscle, Minimum Fat by Ori Hofmekler

- Excellent information on how to lower estrogen, increase growth hormone, optimize testosterone and DHT and much more.

Ageless, by Suzanne Sommers

- Informative compilation of interviews with doctors as well as Suzanne's own take on hormones.

The Testosterone Syndrome, by Eugene Shippen, M.D.

- Very good overview on the importance of testosterone for men as well as the pros and cons of hormone replacement.

The Miracle Of Bio-Identical Hormones, by Michael E Platt, M.D.

- Good review of the pros and cons of bio-identical hormones containing several case studies.

Is Having a Positive
Attitude Overrated?

Self-help gurus often talk about the importance of having a positive attitude, claiming it's fundamental to the success of any and all endeavors. On the contrary - attitude is irrelevant. Couple the brightest of attitudes with a flawed plan and you'll create only failure, while taking that same action with an effective plan (even if your attitude is less than cheerful) you'll surely succeed. Quoting former Navy SEAL Team Six leader Richard Marcinko, you don't have to like it, you just have to do it. Doing what needs to be done even when it's the last thing you want to do, is the critical factor in achieving success.

If you're only capable of taking action when you're attitude is positive, then don't bother. If you require extrinsic motivation to make your move, you should just give up now. If you only perform at a high level when you're feeling your best, then you are the exact opposite of a professional and destined to remain an amateur at life and everything else.

Not only is positive attitude beside the point, it can actually hinder meaningful change as well as ensuing success. I'll share a personal example.

Several years ago, while employed in an especially lame sales job, I learned first-hand the irrelevance of a positive attitude. An idiotic sales manager recommended that to best promote my business I should distribute 500 business cards each day on parked cars. After a few weeks of this, the lack of response left me very disappointed. Now some of you might be thinking a few weeks is nothing and that I needed to demonstrate more commitment and consistency, and while I might agree on principle, I'd argue that a proper marketing plan is the crucial element and that papering people's cars doesn't cut it.

When was the last time a card or flier left on your windshield inspired you to purchase a product or service? Umm, never? But it's a numbers game, you might say - which is exactly what my sales manager said. Further, he convinced me it was my negative attitude killing my card marketing efforts. Wear your biggest smile as you place the cards, he said, and make a positive affirmation as you tuck each card under the wiper. I was young, naive and open minded and I ate up this advice. After all, here was the manager offering me the benefit of his experience, right? I went crazy with the cards. Not only did I paste on an idiotic smile, I kept on smiling as I flipped a record ten thousands cards in a single day. Oh, how excited I was about taking this massive action and how I eagerly anticipated an equally massive response. Unfortunately, the only positive result I saw was increased cardio conditioning from running the parking lots all day.

The only phone calls I received after this marketing fiasco were complaints. One guy told me the card I'd stuck in his driver's side window had worked its way down into the door costing him $500 to remove and that he'd be billing me shortly. Another guy left a message that he'd saved my card and intended to staple it to my forehead. es, all the smiling and positive affirmations were finally bringing me results but, as you can see, it was a crappy marketing plan, not a lack of positive attitude that created this mess.

I shared my frustrations with the manager and his response was classic. He said my attitude was still lacking in that what I'd assumed was a positive attitude was merely a facade. Worse, my underlying negative attitude was apparently so tenacious it had transferred itself to the cards as I placed them on each car!

Einstein himself said the definition of insanity is doing the same thing and expecting different results. Here I'd proven to myself that the card marketing method was worthless. Hey, when you do ten thousand of anything, something positive should come of it! If not, your best efforts might be crippled by a poor plan of action. It took little intellection to realize it was time to try something different.

The number one flaw in card marketing is that it requires an extreme effort to get your word out. Several thousand cards, plus the hours spent distributing those cards, is an exercise in inefficiency. What I needed was a system of promoting my business to vast numbers of people requiring minimal effort. After doing some research, I decided upon signs.

Starting out with fifty signs, I put them up on telephone poles and stakes at major intersections. The best and most efficient way to post signs is in the middle of the night when traffic is low. I'd go out around 2 A.M. in the blistering cold and put up my signs. Did I maintain that all-important positive attitude? Not even close. I was bitching the entire time but I nailed in those signs until the job was done, the sun still coming up and then dragged myself back home to get some sleep. I awoke, several hours later, to more than twenty voice messages from people interested in what I was offering. My closing rate on those callbacks were one in three, which is pretty good. I had finally discovered a method that worked, and despite any semblance of positive attitude during the process, my course of action was met with success.

Take an effective plan, put it into action, have the tenacity to see it through, and it will work in spite of your positive, negative, or indifferent attitude. When it comes to making dramatic, positive change in your life, a positive attitude is the least of your concerns, and in fact, may actually inhibit you in accepting the brutal self-knowledge required to break free of inertia and move forward.

People often tell me about their intense level of dissatisfaction with their jobs, ending with how they stay positive and look on the bright side to avoid feelings of depression and insanity. They'll continue that eventually when the time is right they'll pursue their dream careers. While gratitude for what you have is a good thing, it doesn't mean you should ever accept a life you don't want. Forcing positivity in the face of wrong livelihood is only the illusion of positive. Tricking yourself into feeling good about something bad is only an effective plan for negative outcomes.

Recently, I read a great article about senior citizens looking back over their lives. Naturally, some had regrets about things they'd done over the years, but the strongest regrets were felt for things that weren't ever done.

What does this have to do with positive attitude? A stubborn positive attitude may be the enabling factor in continuing to slog on with a life you don't even want. Sometimes, it's hitting rock bottom that spurs forward action. No, you don't have to lose all your worldly possessions and end up on the street but you do have to feel low-down and angry enough with yourself for accepting your misappropriated life. When you are completely fed up and nauseated at the idea of remaining as you have been, you are finally ready to initiate change and create a new life.

Creation is dramatic and powerful, not passive and subtle. Creation arises from destruction and only by destroying your wrongfully lived life can you finally embrace the life you've always wanted. This is what it means to be reincarnated as a new person. There are no second chances when you're keeping one foot in your old life; your anger and extreme dissatisfaction are the flames that burn the bridges to your past. Dramatic change isn't always pretty, nor does it always come from a pretty, positive place.

In short, putting a positive spin on a negative situation is lying to yourself - and there's nothing positive about lies. Getting a flat tire on the way to an important meeting, you might pull off to the side of the road and think of all the positive reasons that this might have happened. Perhaps in getting a flat you avoided a terrible accident up the road. Maybe the meeting is being held in a building assigned to be blown up by terrorists. With this line of reasoning, you might even thank the stars and feel gratitude for your flat tire - not so fast! As outlandish as it might sound to the positive thinkers among you, your flat tire is probably nothing more than one of the multiple, irritating, inconveniences we all deal with from time to time. The solution? Get out of your car, change the tire, and get back on the road - no positive attitude required. You know what needs to be done, get it done and move on.

You may think a flat tire is a trivial example, so let's use something more compelling. How about pediatric burn victims? As a non-burned person, would you feel comfortable telling these children to stay positive and feel gratitude for what they have? These kids are in the depths of suffering and they are not wrong to feel angry about it. While they must eventually move on from their state of suffering, their healing will come faster by accepting their current, terrible, reality before moving onward. Insisting that everything is fine only defers crucial feelings which need to be brought to awareness.

Terrible things happen all the time to people who don't deserve them and there's nothing positive to be said about it. Not only is it healthy to accept this fact (that some things are indeed negative and even terrible) it's essential to leading a self-realized life. Life is never all-negative nor all-positive. Some things are wonderful, some terrible, and there's no use in struggling over what seems to be duality but in fact is not.

Self-help gurus claim you must feel positive in order to take any right action. They'll have you do drills, like listing all the reasons you should do something, then listing all the reasons not to do it. If your positives out-weigh the negatives, then you should take action. Well, if you even have to make such a list, then your priorities are confused. When you really want something, you form a plan of action and execute it. You don't indulge in mental masturbation. That which is important will obsess you and force you into action.

Far more important than a positive attitude are preparation and sound training. A positive attitude without preparation will lose out. Even with a negative attitude, when matched with training and preparation, you are far more likely to persevere and thrive.

Best of all, by taking the necessary action to acquire the life you really want to live, you'll naturally feel positive feelings about your life. Taking charge of your life is exciting and exhilarating, while lying to yourself about anything, including that which seems positive, is hollow and demoralizing.

So forget about trying to change your attitude! Put together your action plan, get going, and show courage in the face of the inevitable errors and setbacks. You know what you need to do and you don't have to like it, you just have to do it.

THE NECESSITY OF
NEGATIVE THINKING

I do not know about you, but I have had it with self-help gurus that state you should always be positive, no matter what. As we've touched upon in the previous chapter, proponents of positive thinking state that you should always look on the bright side, and that no situation is negative unless you believe it is.

While this line of thinking might sound good in theory, in practice it is a guaranteed way to never achieve your goals or improve your life. Moreover, always looking on the bright side can be used as an excuse for not improving your life, or going after your goals. After all, if everything is great why make any changes?

Contrary to what positive thinking devotees say, applying negative thinking is often necessary to achieve your goals and improve your life. Besides, negative thinking is a necessity in order to avoid making the same mistakes over and over again. Is negative thinking superior to positive thinking? Not necessarily. A balance of both positive and negative energy is necessary for equilibrium. Let's start off by going over some of the pitfalls of positive thinking.

First: Positive thinkers believe that you should always look on the bright side. To some degree, I agree with this. After all, many people dwell on the negative in order to get attention from other people, which is down right pathetic. I have met people that like to show off about their problems as a way to get others to feel sorry for them. These "poor me" addicts are real energy vampires, and you want to avoid such people like the plague. When you offer solutions they immediately dismiss them, they want the problems. Often in life you have to realize, if you don't want the solution then you want the problem.

For most, there will always be people that are far worse off than we are, and we should be grateful for what we have. I have had the good fortune to travel all over the world. I have seen immense suffering, which makes so called suffering in America look like a trip to Disneyland. You definitely feel grateful for what you have after seeing such intense suffering. Regardless, we should not use this line of thinking as an excuse to accept circumstances that are not optimal. If anything, we should use it as a motivational fire, to fully value the opportunities we have and to take full advantage of them. Being positive about things that are negative is not the way to evolve.

For example, lets say that you are broke, overweight, and have no friends. You decide to apply positive thinking and accept your situation. After all, it could always be worse. You tell yourself that you are lucky to be you and you walk around with a smile on your face. You tell yourself that there is no need to make money, make friends, or lose weight because everything is okay as it is. There are a lot of people that are far worse off so you should be grateful for what you have. Is this really addressing the problem?

Do you really believe that someone is genuinely happy in this situation? I don't think so. Lets flip the script and apply some negative thinking to this situation. You decide that you are fed up with being broke, overweight, and lonely. You cannot stand who you are anymore, and the idea of staying the same is nauseating. You get angry and decide to take charge of your life. The dissatisfaction of the situation makes you furious, and you take action immediately. Additionally, you will stay the course, anytime you feel complacent you will think about the life you have to go back to, and that is a very powerful driving force to persevere and push forward.

Without a doubt someone that applies negative thinking in this situation is more likely to achieve his or her goals. Why? Because he or she is in touch with reality, and realizes that calling a lame situation good does not change it in the real world. Sometimes a brutal dose of reality is just the medicine you need to make some serious changes that will result in a positive impact.

Second: Positive thinkers believe that having a positive attitude at all times is the key to success. If you want to make money, then smile at yourself in the mirror and tell yourself that you are already a millionaire and start acting like one. By doing so, you will attract lots of money into your life. Sounds like a great plan. Unfortunately it does not pan out in the real world.

Imagine if you decided that you wanted to bench press 400lbs. You have never done more than 300lbs yet you think that if you just apply enough positive thinking you will be able to bench press 400lbs.

You spend an hour in the mirror telling yourself that you can do it over and over again. Then you hit the gym load up the bar to 400lbs and die an agonizing death when you get pinned. 400lbs does not care if you are positive or not. You could be the biggest jerk in the world, but be able to bench press 400lbs.

Positive thinking will not take the place of training and preparation. Sure, being confident and telling yourself that you can do something is great; if you have put in the honest time and hard work. However, attempting to bypass training and hard work with positive thinking is a recipe for disaster.

Third: Proponents of positive thinking often state that you should forgive people that have screwed you over. Otherwise, you will harbor anger that will negatively affect your life. In some cases this might be true.

For example, if you kill someone or beat him or her to a pulp for not paying you back some money that they owe you, the consequences of your actions will most likely make your life much worse. Also, if you dwell on how someone screwed you over to the point that it consumes your daily thoughts then you are setting yourself up for unhappiness. You are most likely better off putting your energy elsewhere.

That said, just letting it go and doing nothing is going to make you feel like a chump. Someone that applies positive thinking will probably say that they were meant to have the money that you leant them and that they will probably benefit from it, and that you will get good karma in return. Again, sounds good on paper, but it is not that simple in the real world.

If the person is dishonest, and does not pay you back, do you really think that they are going to do something positive with the money? I doubt it. Thus, it is highly unlikely that good energy will come back your way for helping out a loser. You don't have to go after someone who owes you money, but at least admit that someone burned you and get that person out of your life.

Make sure that you tell other people as well, so that they do not get screwed over. Admitting that you got screwed over will at least prevent you from making the same mistake again.

Lying to yourself, and telling yourself that you never made a mistake, will just cause you to make the same mistakes over and over again. Some of our greatest lessons come from our mistakes. There is no need to avoid admitting that you made a mistake to be positive. Learning from a mistake is a positive action to take. Famous rapper Jay-Z once said in an interview, that he only learns from his mistakes, and that it is not possible for him to learn from his successes. This is a very powerful statement from a very successful man. The key is to actually admit you made a mistake and avoid making the same mistake over and over again. Yes, we can learn a lot more from our mistakes, than our successes.

Fourth: Proponents of positive thinking believe in the benefits of affirmations. For example, if you have a fear of public speaking, just tell yourself over and over again that you can do it and that you are already a great speaker. Sorry, affirmations will not make up for experience. If you have never done any public speaking then expect to be terrible at it when you begin. Hell, be prepared to be terrible at if for a long time if not indefinitely. You will only get better with deliberate practice and lots of it.

In the beginning you will be terrible, but if you do it often enough and actually put concerted effort into improving, you will become more comfortable and get better. Several years ago I had to give a sales presentation to a group of prospects. I had some trepidation about doing it, but told myself over and over that I would be great.

To make a long story short, I got in front of the group and went blank. I started sweating profusely as I tried to remember what I wanted to say but could not remember anything. My supervisor had to come up and save me. It was humiliating and I got angry. I had to do another sales presentation the following week and this time I prepared, and did a good job.

The humiliation of screwing up in front of my peers motivated me to get better. I accepted the fact that I was terrible and that I needed to practice and prepare for the next presentation. If I just told myself that I did fine, I would have screwed up again and again.

Affirmations will never make up for real world practice and a reality check. Being positive can make you comfortable and cause you to avoid improving. If you already believe you are good at something why take the time to improve? You have to accept where you are, to go where you want to go.

At this point you are probably thinking that positive thinking is complete garbage. Well, it really depends on how you define positive thinking. I do no think that being positive is garbage. Sure, it is a good idea to believe in yourself, take chances, and have a positive outlook on life.

We have all been around people that are cynical and negative about everything and they are a real drain to be around. However, people that are ecstatic about everything, such as the singer Celine Dion, can also be extremely irritating.

Life is both positive, and negative, and attempting to deny either is unrealistic. The key is to know when to apply what. Be positive when things are going well. When things are not going well, admit it and use negative energy to change it. Negative energy meaning anger, irritation, frustration, and dissatisfaction.

Dissatisfaction will cause you to get angry, and anger can be a powerful force to improve your life. We don't strive to evolve and improve when we think everything is going great. We strive to evolve when we are dissatisfied. Being dissatisfied is often a critical component of success and happiness. It is what gets you to quit soulless jobs, or get out of destructive relationships.

If you really want to be positive then you have to learn how to be negative as well. The key is to be in the middle. If you are negative all of the time you will end up in the same place as people that are positive all the time. That place is the land of mediocrity.

People that are super negative blame everyone but themselves for all of their problems, while people that are super positive believe that they do not have any room for improving and evolving. Both people are in illusion land and are handicapped by their thinking. You have to be in the middle, so if you are a super positive thinker, then it is time to get that stupid smile off your face!

Stop wasting time thinking that your pathetic life is great, and do something right now to change it. On the other hand, if you are a super negative cynic, then stop blaming the world for all of your problems and take responsibility for your life!

THE DANGER OF
ALWAYS ACCOMMODATING

I don't think you were put here to please everybody; that would be horrible.
You have to have some kind of a stand and stand against something as well.
If not, you're just being accommodating.

-- Rocco Deluca

A few years ago I was talking to my friend, Harley Flanagan, about a DVD project on fat loss. As you may know, Harley's the founder of the NYC hardcore band, The Cro-Mags, and is working on a new CD (which I'm financing) that'll be out soon. I've heard some of it and it rocks! But that's a story for another time, so let's get back to the conversation I had with Harley. While Harley likes my DVD, he thinks I'm missing the mainstream market with my personality and teaching style. He didn't insult my approach, just stated that it's hardcore and intimidating to a lot of people. He's probably right, but me making a soft, mainstream fitness DVD is like asking Harley to model his musical style after Justin Timberlake in order to hit the mainstream market! It is not going to happen! It means not being genuine, and when you're not genuine people pick up on it. This is a main reason why most fitness DVDs and most music Cd's are terrible: instead of doing what he wants to do and letting it flow authentically, the artist starts thinking about what's going to sell and how to please people. Hell, this is the main reason why most movies are forgettable: too much of a corporate cookie-cutter approach that insults the viewer. You know what's going to

37

happen in the first ten minutes and thus drift into oblivion for the next two hours.

The problem with being accommodating is the focus gets shifted to what doesn't matter. In an episode of Inside the Actor's Studio, actor Matt Damon said that winning an Academy Award shouldn't be the focus of an actor, rather, the focus should be the craft itself and doing the best job possible. The best job possible comes from being genuine, and in the moment, instead of being focused on graining the approval of others.

The problem with always accommodating the needs of others is you stop taking risks, and begin to live your life like a spineless politician who has to take a poll before any decision. If you only take action after getting validation from others, then you'll never live fully. You're no longer a real person, but a pinball in the game of life being thrown from one side of the table to the other - not an empowering way to live, to say the least. There's a rush that comes from having the deck stacked against you and prevailing; those are the times when you discover what you're made of and are fully alive.

Many of the greatest human beings were people who refused to be quiet and accommodate the wishes of others. Gandhi refused to move from his seat on a train and as a result was literally thrown off the train. He went from being a lawyer focused on making money to becoming arguably the greatest human rights leader of all time. Gandhi learned the importance of not accommodating in seemingly insignificant cases and used that to prepare himself for the major cases later in his life.

Being accommodating in major areas of your life comes from being accommodating in the seemingly insignificant areas. Recently, I was on a flight and got stuck in the middle of a row. Not a fun place to be, and even worse when you're seated between a couple talking over you while passing things back and forth to each other. It was irritating and disrespectful, to say the least. Finally, I suggested that I either switch seats with one of them or they respect my personal space and stop passing things over me and talking over me.

While they were the ones that were being rude, both of them looked at me like I was crazy. Clearly they were used to having their way. Fortunately I spotted an empty window seat in the front row and moved leaving the annoying couple pondering why someone had the audacity to question their rude and inconsiderate actions.

Yes, I realize the above instance of non-accommodation is hardly dramatic. But, that's the point: it starts with the small stuff. When you accommodate others, you're a victim and as a result, no matter how insignificant the situation you create a victim pattern. If you can't stand your ground with small stuff, you'll be crushed when major events come your way, e.g., instead of quitting a lame job and going after what you really want, you'll accommodate the boss, taking the path of least resistance. In this manner, your entire life passes you by with you wondering what happened.

From an early age we're taught to accommodate others at the expense of ourselves. Sure, some accommodation is necessary and we can't always have things our way, but letting others walk all over us and decide how we should live our lives isn't acceptable. You don't have to explain your actions to others nor get their approval. So some people aren't going to like you? Well, they weren't going to like you anyway so it's not a big deal.

It's a liberating feeling knowing you don't have to take crap from people; you can stand your ground and do what's best for you instead of living a fear-based, accommodating lifestyle. Just remember to be a non-accommodator with the small stuff and you'll automatically become a non-accommodator with the major battles.

Don't Rely on
Your Illusory Memory

The elaborate tapestry of our experience is not stored in memory — at least not in its entirety. Rather, it is compressed for storage by first being reduced to a few critical threads, such as a summary phrase ("Dinner was disappointing"). Later, when we want to remember our experience, our brains quickly reweave the tapestry by fabricating--not by actually retriev-ing--the bulk of the information that we experience as memory. This fabrication happens so quickly and effortlessly that we have the illusion that the entire thing was in our heads the entire time.

— *Daniel Gilbert, author of* Stumbling On Happiness

One of the main reasons people don't learn from their experiences is because their memories of what happened are inaccurate. The memory of what actually occurred can be so distant from truth that the memory is worthless as a learning tool thus the same mistakes are repeated over and over. So much for experience and wisdom going hand and hand!

I experienced this firsthand when reviewing the film footage for one of my fitness DVD projects The Boys Are Back In Town. Some of the footage surprised me, for example, the final panel discussion was much different than I remembered: My memory was that when asked a question I'd get to the point quickly, but in reality I went on big tangents, taking forever to get to the point! Needless to say, that footage didn't make the cut. This experience was extremely helpful and every workshop since I've applied the "less is more" concept. At least that's what I think I'm doing... according to my fabricated memories

The concept of subjectively fabricating our memories brings to mind an episode from a popular 80's sitcom Different Strokes. In the episode, members of the television family are victims of a robbery and a visiting police officer interviews each family member to report what happened. The problem is, each family member has a vastly different memory of what took place. Each family member recalls his or her own brave actions throughout the robbery while remembering everyone else as petrified with fear. This is another example of the mind's trickery: putting all our actions into a positive context to support, and even justify, those actions. By the end of the episode, the police officer realizes each family member's testimony is worthless. What really happened is up for grabs, even the people who were present don't know.

Another reason for our faulty memories is a tendency to recall, and interpret, events in order to meet the expectations of others, e.g., we see something and may classify it as "terrible" but if popular opinion names it acceptable, we'll file it away in our minds as "acceptable". One of my favorite shows, M.A.S.H., aired an episode regarding just such mental fabrication. On the show, the main character, Hawkeye, fondly recalls his memories of growing up with his cousin. Hawkeye remembers his cousin as mentor and close friend; however, after probing further into his memory with the help of a psychologist, Hawkeye recalls his cousin's attempt to drown him by forcing his head underwater and holding it there. Pulling him out of the water at the last minute, the cousin has the audacity to inform Hawkeye he's just saved his life! Hawkeye's family thinks the cousin is a great guy and loves him, so rather then telling his father what really happened, Hawkeye accepts a mental fabrication that his cousin saved his life instead of attempting to drown him. Yet the truth was stored deep in his subconscious mind and destined to surface in the future. Sometimes we find truth too difficult to accept because it could shatter our worldview. Rather than facing it as is, we process it into something we find more agreeable. Then we'll push the truth into the back of our minds, filed away within stacks of do-not-open boxes.

While the truthful memories are stored away in the subconscious mind and therefore not easily accessible, our refined, easy-to-digest fabrications are kept readily at-hand, ready to feed our self-delusions.

Over many years of providing people with online training services, I've realized the best way to get people on track and keep them there is by insisting they keep training journals. When the client's goals are losing fat or putting on size, nutrition journals are also critical. A recent study of 685 people showed that subjects who kept accurate diet journals lost twice as much weight than those who didn't.

What is so magical about writing things down? Assuming you're honest and keeping a detailed journal, your journal keeps those truths in front of you. This means you record your food intake immediately to ensure accuracy, i.e., after eating breakfast you write down every single thing you ate. Cream and sugar in your coffee? If yes, you'll record it promptly and later do the calorie total and a macro nutrient breakdown for each meal.

If you "cheat" (maybe you have a Snickers while driving to work) you write it down. After a week of keeping a detailed diet journal the truth is in front of you. You'll understand why you're not losing weight and can make the necessary modifications to get on track. Relying on memory is a delusional no-brainer, people tend to recall only their healthy food choices any given day. My online clients are shocked when they review their daily food logs and tally calorie numbers. I've had people estimate their daily caloric intake at 2000 calories only to discover they are, in fact, consuming 3500 calories...or more. I've had clients describe their sugar consumption as "insignificant" when in truth it was "colossal".

Remember, for your journal to be accurate (and therefore, useful) you must record your food intake as soon as it goes down. Don't make the common mistake of waiting for the end of the day, then relying upon a faulty memory to summarize the day's meals - your journal is sure to be inaccurate. Yes, this means you must carry a pen and notebook (or other recording device) at all times. A nuisance, you say? Sure it is. You can always opt, as most people do, to remain overweight. You have your choice of burdens: either carry a pen and notebook along everywhere and record your meals or continue humping around fifty extra pounds of fat. You have free will to decide which is the bigger nuisance. Hopefully, your decision won't be colored by fabricated, faulty memories, justifications, or outright lies.

Dietary indiscretions aside, another subject regarding our flawed memories to which most of us can relate is credit card statements. We receive our monthly credit card statement and are shocked by the balance. We think there must be a mistake, scrutinizing each expenditure, knowing that certainly we couldn't possibly have spent so much money. After adding everything up, we discover the statement is correct, and worse, just because we don't remember spending the money, doesn't mean we didn't. Overspending with a credit card is tantamount to overeating. Most people don't bother keeping track of either, thus finding themselves fat and broke. Unpleasant, perhaps, but an honest assessment.

Another arena requiring detailed record keeping is running your own (successful) business. Imagine relying on memory to recall the money made and spent each month! This is an effective way to go out of business very quickly. Ask me how I know. This is how I ran my previous business many years ago. I was so busy trying to drum up business each day that I didn't bother keeping track of how much actual income I was generating. Since I was always so busy, always working hard, I deluded myself into believing I was making money. Well, why wouldn't I be making money? I was working my ass off and we all know hard work goes hand-in-hand with money-making, right? When, finally, I calculated my income against my expenditures, the truth right there became obvious: I was not only earning nothing, I was going further into debt each month keeping a defective business afloat.

Fortunately, I learned a tough lesson from an otherwise meaningless business venture. Meaningless because it didn't represent me, nor what I wanted to do with my life. My current work, on the other hand, is meaningful and one factor that allowed me to build my successful business is accurate accounting. I can tell you exactly, right now, my income - down to the cents and no, this isn't in my head, rather, it's in a detailed business journal.

When you know your exact number, there is a natural human drive to improve it. The context doesn't matter: whether you're trying to lose fat, gain muscular size and strength, or make more money, you need to know your number. When you know it, you'll work hard and amass creative energy to improve it. When you remain ignorant of your number, you're inclined to rely on fabricated memories, or worse, lies.

Our memories are insufficient, and potentially only as real as the movies which entertain us. Making an honest, accurate assessment of yourself may seem depressing, but truth, in all its forms, is nothing less than beautiful. What's depressing is lying to yourself and choosing to remain in the matrix of your mind.

NETWORKING MYTHS!
IT IS MORE THAN WHO YOU KNOW

Networking is important to succeed in business endeavors...but when it comes to effective networking, most people blow it. In this article, I'm going to outline two common networking blunders: one I refer to as premature networking and the other, nuisance networking.

We'll begin with premature networking. Not only do I receive frequent emails from premature networkers, I've met more premature networkers in person then I care to remember. What is premature networking? It's trying to work with people out of your league before earning the right to work with such people. An example is trying to get a face-to-face meeting with Warren Buffet on how to be a millionaire when you haven't even made your first thousand dollars. Even if you manage to pull off the meeting, you're still not ready to benefit from Buffet's information. An analogy is those people who've never taught a workshop offering to co-present a workshop with me.

On my own, I've presented more than one hundred successful workshops, and when I say on my own I mean I did everything from writing the ad copy; promoting the course; booking the facilities; taking registrations; and leading the courses. Trust me, it's not easy juggling all these aspects, and if you've never done it on your own, you haven't earned the privilege to headline with those who have.

A smarter approach is volunteering to assist at a course you've already taken, or a course covering a subject in which you're already competent. Even better is to present your own workshop! After you've experienced success on your own, you'll find people are more inclined to work with you. Sounds easy, right? Wrong - which is why most people remain premature networkers; they desire easy success, starting with passing the buck onto others. This flawed strategy will only take you so far. Most premature networkers won't ever make it to first base. Successful people won't touch a premature "pass-the-buck" networker, and can spot them a mile away.

Another aspect of premature networking is developing a list of contacts without anything to offer them. I knew a guy in Los Angeles who wanted to become a famous actor. He was a great networker and knew many famous actors but what are they going to do for him if he has nothing to offer? You guessed it: nothing. His daily routine of four hours of television viewing, plus trying to get laid, left him little time to seriously pursue the actor's craft and, in the end, thirty years of living in LA added up to very little. Such stories are a dime a dozen in LA, which leads in to the next example, someone who's never written a script but has an idea that he can schedule a pitch and meeting like a professional script writer. This pass-the-buck networking is so irritating it segues nicely into my next subject, nuisance networking.

Yes, the next logical networking category people blunder into is nuisance networking. These are those people who literally bother other people. An example is those who bombard others with emails seeking free information. These are people thinking only of themselves without respect for other people's time. When meeting someone new, they instantly size you up to see if you'll meet some self-serving purpose. A nobler approach is leading in with how you might benefit that person with whom you're attempting to network. Along these lines, an especially effective networking approach I've had success with is the interview.

Interviewing those people whom you'd like to work with, and learn from, is effective networking. It works well because you're leading with an opportunity for them rather than for you. Trying to get other people to do stuff for you without emphasizing the benefit to them is losing a battle without ever getting started. Leading in with a benefit to the contact gets your foot in the door, and an excellent chance of crossing the threshold! When I originally contacted people for interviews, I mentioned only that I'd like to interview them for a particular publication. I identified myself as a freelance writer and included some examples of my published work. Most of these samples were online articles, which are relatively easy to get published since so many sites are looking for content.

Rather than emailing people with bothersome requests for free information (i.e., nuisance networking) I sent brief notes detailing the benefits of an interview and waited for their response. It was a numbers game: plenty of people said no (or never replied, which is another version of no) but several did get back to me. In fact, in my first month, I interviewed MMA legend Frank Shamrock; Richard Machowicz (author of Unleashing the Warrior Within and host of Future Weapons); fitness expert Clarence Bass; top strength coach Tudor Bompa; and top strength coach Steve Maxwell.

In addition to leveraging their names to get my name out there, I learned a great deal from each of them - not only from the interviews but by developing some solid relationships. I did a good job with the interviews, getting their final approval before sending them in for publication, and I never pitched any of these men on kettlebell training, hiring me as a trainer, working together on workshops, or trying to get them to do any stuff for me at all. I opened with an offer to do something for them and delivered on my offer, which creates the strong foundation upon which relationships are built. For example, a few years after my interview with Frank Shamrock, I met him in person and presented a seminar at his gym. He was so impressed with the seminar he didn't hesitate to offer me a powerful testimonial. Timing is crucial: if I'd asked Frank for endorsement too soon, he would have - justifiably - blown me off. Why would he endorse someone he's never met? Further, without knowing anything about me, why would he agree to host my seminar at his gym?

To effectively network, lead with an offer to the other party, then patiently allow the relationship to grow organically. You can't force things, solid networking takes time and the more value you have to offer, the more effective your networking opportunities. If you have nothing to offer, you're just hanging out and networking is more than attending seminars and other events to chitchat with people.

The bottom line: you can learn from people without ever meeting them. You want to know how I run my business and how I get things done? It's all on my website. You can learn to write effective ad copy by analyzing what I've already written. It's right there in front of you and you don't need me to tutor you. Nor am I available for tutoring. You can find a book on any topic you can imagine, but are you prepared to read twenty-five books on how to achieve success in your chosen field? If your answer is no, choose another field. Twenty-five books is the minimum you should read about something for which you allege a passion.

Finally, yes, networking is important - but both premature networking and nuisance networking are wastes of time and will only succeed in ruining your reputation as word gets around. In order to effectively network, develop an honest skill in order to offer something of value in the marketplace - and to those people with whom you wish to network. Create a win-win situation and respect people's time.

DON'T EVER GET INVOLVED WITH NETWORK MARKETING COMPANIES

Self-help Gurus often recommend network-marketing companies as your ticket to financial freedom and liberation. Nothing could be further from the truth and you should avoid networking marketing companies like the bubonic plague!

I hate networking marketing companies aka multi-level marketing (MLM) or, more appropriately, pyramid schemes. Amway is the most common network marketing company (Also disguised as quixtar which is a part of Amway), and the one by which probably everyone in the world has been pitched. Now, what is it that I hate so much about network marketing? Is it the products? Some MLM companies actually sell decent products, albeit always overpriced and dependent upon aggressive distributors pressing those products on suffering friends and family members, this being the second-most irritating aspect of network marketing. The number one most irritating aspect is the focus on "building" an organization. Let's take a further look.

When you join a network marketing company you'll typically be signed up by someone referred to as your "sponsor". Sometimes, this sponsor acts as a "mentor" and other times they're just a name and that's the end of it. You're better off with the latter, since the former sees you only through the dollar signs obstructing his eyes, hoping you're a hard working and tenacious individual. Your "mentor" hopes to find as many hard-working people as possible to build up his organization. Why? Because the more work you do, the less work he does.

The first thing your sponsor will do is ask for a list of everyone you know. Your sponsor will further ask you to call each person on your list, pitching the company's products and a business "opportunity". And it gets better: your mentor will sit in on each call with you, the better to perform a shameful tag-team, hard-sell to the unfortunate on the receiving end. To illustrate this process, let's use a network marketing company selling weight-loss products...the pitch goes something like this:

YOU: I just started my own company and I've got some great weight loss products to tell you about! (MLM people always refer to the company as "their" company, which is a losing combination of pathetic and hysterical.)

YOU: Do you know anyone who'd like to lose 10-30 pounds in thirty days?

(This is known as the indirect pitch. Really, what you're telling your Aunt Millie is she's a fat ass who should buy some of these overpriced products. Worse, you're actually hoping to get her not only buying product but making a list of her own prospects to call and pitch. Down the road, you want these fat people distributing beneath you and repeating the same process with everyone they know.)

Your sponsor will tell you you're not "selling" your friends, no, you're simply sharing your enthusiasm. Most people hate selling and wouldn't ever want to do it for a living, much less huckster their friends and family. For this reason, your network mentor must convince you that you're not a salesperson; you're simply a satisfied customer wanting to share your enthusiasm with others. An analogy will be made to seeing a great movie and, naturally, telling all your friends and family about it. Maybe you'd do that, but that's not analogous to calling the people you most care about and selling your lame product or - still lame - a business opportunity. First, there's no profit in your friends going to see your enthused-about movie. Once money enters the picture it's no longer innocent enthusiasm: you now have an ulterior motive and if you think otherwise, you're in conflict with reality. Of course there is nothing wrong with selling products. It is trying to hide the fact that you are selling products that is irritating.

As lame as pitching your friends and family on over-priced and hyped-up products is, network marketing will press you on towards still darker territory. Fact: your network-marketing goal isn't selling a lot of product. No, your true goal is getting other people selling as much product as possible and, in turn, recruiting still others to do the same.

Network marketing is thus the ultimate pass-the-buck game. Your sponsor recruits you so she won't have to work. You, in turn, recruit others so you won't have to work. Everyone keeps passing the buck along, hoping a hard worker eventually arrives so everyone else can take it easy. Your ultimate goal is an organization full of hard working, hard-selling people making you tons of money. While these people don't earn much individually, enough of them, each selling a little bit, adds up. Why would anyone work so hard, for so little reward, in network marketing? For this illusion: that someday you'll become a millionaire like the top performers in the company. Reality: You're more likely to get struck by lightening (or receive an unlimited pass to the Playboy Mansion) than become a millionaire via network marketing.

Once you've sold a few products as a network marketer, your sponsor will ask you to make another list of people to pitch. This time, you'll pitch them on not only product, but on joining the business. Any income story will do, thus if you made $25.00 selling product, that's the income story your sponsor will tell you to lead with. It might go something like this:

YOU: Hey, I just started my own business and just today I made $25.00 - do you know anyone who'd like to make an extra $500.00 to $1500.00 per month? (Again, the indirect pitch - and also a number to which most people can relate. If you ask someone if they know anyone who'd like to make an extra $50,000 a month, they'll think either

    a)   You're dealing drugs, or
    b)   The whole thing is a joke

Suggesting an extra $500.00 a month sounds more tangible and is therefore a stronger hook.)

Nevertheless, the response on the other end is sure to be hesitation and reluctance. Since nobody wants anything to do with sales, your sponsor will tell you to use the same pitch she used on you:

YOU: It's not sales, it's customer service and sharing your enthusiasm.

All you have to do is use the products and share your excitement. Sure, just get "excited" about products and then tell everyone...sounds like a plot from Fantasy Island.

Given network marketing's bad reputation, why would any company choose it as a distribution system? The benefits are numerous. One, you needn't pay to advertise your products - all your distributors who pay to work for you do that. Two, you'll acquire a sales force (of potentially thousands) who'll work without benefits. No employee hassles and no paying out medical benefits. Better than developing a high-quality, professional sales team, offer an illusory opportunity to as many people as possible and hope you'll get a few winners to stick around. Even better, once you get your core distributors lined up, the process goes viral, meaning the distributors already installed do the work of recruiting more salespeople to peddle the products.

Another negative aspect of network marketing as a distribution system is the high percentage of profit paid out per sale. When a distributor makes a sale, he gets a cut of the action and several people above him get a cut of the action as well - so if the product isn't grievously overpriced, the company will fold in no time. This is why networking marketing products are priced so much higher than comparable products sold through regular retail. It's the ultimate middleman system with its hierarchy of mark-ups between seller and buyer.

Nor is recruiting friends and family the only way network markets bring in new people. Another common practice is the opportunity meeting. Those in the know refer to this as the deception meeting. Here's how it works: network marketing recruiters place ads in newspapers under the "Jobs" classification (rather than the business opportunity section). The recruiters advertise network-marketing opportunities as "customer service" positions for which there is an hourly wage paid. People calling to inquire about a job are invited to an interview. Once they show up, they're directed to another room for a "group interview". Once there, they're pitched on the "opportunity". At the end of the meeting, they meet with the person who invited them in for the interview to hear more about the opportunity and discuss how much it will cost to begin working. Ever heard of a job for which you pay a fee to start working? Of course not, then again, network marketing isn't a job at all but a world of shady business opportunists.

Some will argue there's nothing wrong with network marketing and it's a great opportunity for supplemental, or even passive income. Then why the need for deception? Why hard-sell your friends, even lying to get them to your opportunity meetings? The bottom line? Few people are willing to join a pyramid scheme, so they must be misdirected. Nobody is willing to do sales so you must deceive them into thinking something else is going on, something like "customer service" or "sharing enthusiasm". The bottom line: network marketing works only for people willing to wear blinders, i.e., people especially good at lying to themselves.

As lame as network marketing is, it's not as bad as it was. Not long ago, distributors were forced to stockpile inventory, often thousands of dollars worth, in order to get reasonable wholesale prices and make their percentage off recruits, otherwise known as your down line. In fact, there's probably enough unsold networking marketing product piled high in garages near you to build a thousand Walmarts! Eventually, network marketing companies started getting sued and a new law was passed to protect consumers. The law requires any network marketing company to purchase back unsold product from any distributor wanting to get out of the business.

I get pitched all the time by network marketers and, from what I can see, most network marketing companies no longer require distributors to stockpile inventory. Most transactions these days take place on the Internet and orders are shipped directly from the parent company to the consumer. That's a step in the right direction but the aim of network marketing remains the same: not selling product personally but recruiting others to make those sales, and the products continue to be grossly overpriced and over-hyped.

There's nothing wrong with selling products you believe in and, obviously, I myself am in the business of selling fitness products. However, I've never held deceptive meetings in order to sell products nor harassed any of my friends or family members. I freely give high-quality information, demonstrating value and building customer trust. My website is positioned to attract people who are interested in what I'm offering. I have no need to talk to everyone I meet about what it is I do. When I go to parties I neither pitch anyone nor do I have a business card (in fact, I don't believe in them). I invite friends over to socialize, not to sell my DVDs and workshops. There's a correct way of conducting business, effective both in the short and long run, and a wrong way of doing business, which may produce results short-term but guarantees long-term disaster.

Remember: there are times when a network marketing pitch is useful. For instance, if you have people hanging around that you want to get rid of, pitch them on a network marketing business, it's the surest way to clear a room or silence incoming phone calls. Next time someone wants to borrow money or otherwise waste your time, tell them you have a great business opportunity you'd like to share with them and get ready for the dial tone. In fact, next time a telemarketer calls you, why not have some fun and pitch him on a network marketing business opportunity? At the least, you'll never hear from them again.

WHY YOUR NEED FOR
PRAISE IS HOLDING YOU BACK

Self help gurus know that most people are addicted to praise. They lure you into their messages by assuring you that you will receive praise all day long if you follow their recommendations. They never reveal the pitfalls of praise and why you should aspire to something greater.

Praise is one of the most addictive and potentially destructive drugs around. OK, maybe it's not that bad, but it can be annihilative to personal growth. As the saying goes: praise is something children cry for and grown people die for. There's nothing wrong with giving or receiving genuine praise; we all appreciate praise for hard work and genuine accomplishment, but it's a mistake to make praise an objective. Praise is a given when doing anything impressive, so focus on executing meaningful actions; perform great feats and praise follows. And if the praise never comes? So what! Achieving greatness is a real reward, not the fickle approval of people you already know or will never know. Further, if people criticize your accomplishments it doesn't mean your accomplishments were without merit. Negative feedback is often praise couched in petty jealousies.

Back to the topic of praise: Most people are unaware of my proudest accomplishments (and no, they've nothing to do with either my training or training business) nor do I care whether anyone knows these things, since the reward of doing them has been more than enough.

The need to report your achievements to anyone and everyone in order to garner praise and significance indicates your actions are about as uninteresting as your personality. Hey, if you don't even impress yourself, don't go looking for outsiders to pick up the slack.

Yet, at the end of the day, praise is merely one of the many reassurances people desperately seek. People broadcast their accomplishments because they can then feel superior. We all know people like this, they're the men and women who always want the focus on them and what they've done. If you talk to such people, they'll cut you off mid-sentence, interrupting with their two cents. They can't listen to you because their minds are occupied only with what they want to say next.

They need to get over themselves! There will always be someone more impressive than yourself so forget about trying to be better than others and focus on improving yourself. Take solace in growing as a person and making day-to-day gains.

Some people require pats on the back in order to stay the course when chasing their goals. This is a sign you lack the necessary seriousness to realize your objectives. Who cares about a pat on the back over real opportunity for personal development? There are many people performing inspiring actions every single day who never receive praise or encouragement yet keep their momentum. Are their actions less important because they're not acknowledged? I don't think so.

Ironically, praise can actually hamper perseverance and thus, growth. My Dad recently sent me an article asserting that praising children for their natural talents is a big mistake. For example, if a child has a natural aptitude for math, laying on thick praise is a big mistake. Why? It discourages children from taking on challenges. Assuming that other areas of life should equally be as effortless, when adversity comes their way, they may see it as a sign to retreat. I don't think adults are any different. Many adults simply focus on things at which they are already adept and never want to take on any challenge. Were they conditioned this way as children? Whatever the reason, such people need to move on to new skills and interests.

Worse, praise givers may simply be attention-seekers. After all, when praised, the recipient is now obligated to acknowledge the source of this praise. I repeat, there is nothing wrong with genuine praise, but you must differentiate between heartfelt praise and ass kissing - and a fine illustration of the latter is Henry Rollins on The Henry Rollins Show. (Now I will interject that I'm a big fan of the band Black Flag, and as some of you may know, Henry Rollins was the lead singer for Black Flag.) I also like what he did with his later project, The Rollins Band. So when I heard Henry had his own show in which he'd be interviewing interesting people and hosting music, I couldn't wait to check it out.

I watched a few episodes of The Henry Rollins Show and it failed to engage me. After a few more viewings I realized why: Henry may talk loud and tough during his weekly rants, but if you listen to what he's saying there's zero controversy or originality. In fact, there's no substance whatsoever, just him bitching like he's post-estrogen booster shot. Unfortunately, his weekly rants are the least of the show's pathetic-ness. His sycophantic behavior with each and every guest is nausea-inducing. For me, the tipping point was an interview with William Shatner. While I'm the first to say Shatner was the best Star Trek captain of all time, that's not where Rollins was going. Nope, he actually praised Shatner for his great music! Anyone who's sampled Shatner's discography knows the horror. I'd rather listen to my dogs bark all night.

There is a comedic value to the recordings since you can't help but laugh your ass off upon listening. Next, Rollins went on to admit that he has all Shatner's records and they continued a discussion of the musical process and how Shatner comes up with his great material. You've got to be kidding me! Delving into William Shatner on musical creativity is like asking Daffy duck about public speaking technique. Hilariously, even Henry Rollins' guests squirm in discomfort when subjected to such artificial praise. Johnny Knoxville was compelled to counter Henry's fawning by replying that even he - Johnny - thought most of his own movies sucked! Now that was funny. Remember: if you are looking for methods to refine your ass kissing, check out Henry's show. The single highlight from the first season was a musical performance by Slayer - even Henry couldn't mess that up.

Back to the topic of praise: balance is key. Live your life without seeking praise from others; praise is illusory, fleeting, but becoming a great person is not. Give genuine praise to others when the opportunity arises, but avoid surgically attaching your head to their ass. No worthwhile person feels flattered by empty praise; great people do great things for their own sake, not for some transient accolades or even pats on the back.

ARE WE BECOMING A NATION OF ORTHOREXICS?

Indeed, no people on earth worry more about the health consequences of their food choices than we Americans do-and no people suffer from as many diet-related health problems. We are becoming a nation of orthorexics: people with an unhealthy obsession with healthy eating.

— Michael Pollan, author of In Defense Of Food

Is there really an epidemic of Americans frantically worrying about what to eat, or is the above statement a gross exaggeration? Junk food manufacturers, including Mickey D's, sure aren't losing any business and the endless lines at the local Las Vegas all-you-can-eat buffets are overflowing with over-eaters at-the-ready. There are more junk foods than ever before while real food is pushed to the corners of supermarkets in order to make more room for more artificial junk. I can't help looking at people's shopping carts when I'm at the store and from what I've seen, I think Americans aren't worrying enough about what it is they're eating (and worse, what they're feeding their children) and the consequences are obvious. Americans worry too much in general, but it doesn't seem to affect their food choices.

With the abundance of information on health and nutrition these days, you'd think we'd have better results. Or maybe that's the problem: when it comes to diet and nutrition, we're beyond information overload. It's easy to empathize with people feeling frustrated and at a loss about which course to take. There exist more diet books than you could possibly read in a lifetime, yet few are worth reading. There are more nutrition supplements on the shelves than ever before, and for every problem you might think of, yet a very few worth taking. In addition to the bombardment of nutrition information, so much of it conflicts that it's no wonder people stress out about food. People get overwhelmed, eat whatever is convenient, and then hope everything turns out okay.

I see people all the time jumping from one diet plan to the next, hoping to one day discover their holy grail of nutrition. One week, they're eating five times a day, then an expert says five meals is no good, three is fine; then another expert says three meals is too many - one meal is the way to go. These experts insist breakfast is the most important meal of the day while those experts argue a big breakfast ruins your whole day's energy. This expert declares cereal the optimal breakfast food, while that expert pronounces cereal mere processed garbage and that fresh fruit is the way to go! There are experts saying we should eat only raw foods while other experts are swearing vegetables must be cooked for us to assimilate their nutrients. This group thinks low-carb is best; another group thinks low fat is critical to good health. I'm getting a headache as I write this and I'm in the health and nutrition field!

It really is enough to drive you crazy. Ironically, among the well-intentioned, health-conscious people out there worrying about the best foods to eat, the elevated cortisol levels resulting from neurotic eating are probably doing worse damage than any actual junk food consumption. Well, maybe I'm exaggerating, but it's pretty damn bad. Sure, focusing on healthy food is the correct action, most of the time, but worrying all day long about what you're going to eat won't in any way increase your health. Surprisingly, eating unhealthy food from time to time won't take years off your life, nor will it ruin your health and nutrition program, yet chronic preoccupation with so-called correct eating may harm your wellness program.

While a growing segment of the American population may becoming increasingly neurotic about what to eat, I doubt Americans' epic, surging cortisol levels comes from their health preoccupations. Most Americans maintain they're overweight from over consuming food that, were they to feed it to their dogs, would get them arrested on charges of animal cruelty. These people aren't worrying about eating too much! But, these same people can and do experience a sense of guilt over their eating habits which manifests as a sickening cycle of eating junk, feeling bad about it, then eating more junk in a pathological attempt at feeling better. Recognize anyone? Should you give in to peer pressure and do as everyone else does? If not, how to get started with intelligent eating?

Are you someone for whom food has become not a fuel for living but instead a versatile and readily available drug-of-choice? When you feel lonely, do you distract yourself by eating a favorite snack? Got fired from work today? Soothe yourself with some ice cream. Feeling sad? Eat some junk food for a little pick-me-up. Feeling great? Celebrate with your favorite foods and live it up! There are always reasons to eat another meal and even ways to rationalize eating whatever it is you want. Do you even know what true hunger feels like? Do you eat by the clock or use hunger as a cue?

I promote personal responsibility and encourage people to take charge of their lives. While I know in my heart people know better than to eat garbage all day long, I concede there is plenty of conflicting, confusing information out there. Yet most nutrition experts agree: better to focus on real food, not packaged garbage. This part isn't complicated: when you go grocery shopping, stay out of the middle of the store. Walk into the grocery store, then turn right and work your way along the perimeter - that's where you'll find the real food. That doesn't mean all the foods along the edge are either real or healthy - no! That's just where the majority of real, healthy foods are displayed. Nor is everything in the middle of the store bad: frozen fruits and vegetables are good options when you're on a budget or shop infrequently.

Healthy eating isn't as complicated as you think. The key is focusing on real foods, not man-made varieties. Hint: if it comes in box listing dozens of ingredients you can't pronounce, it's not real food. Eat healthy most of the time, and then enjoy a once-weekly "cheat day" in which you eat whatever you like, guilt free. According to Joel Marion (my friend, and author of The Cheater's Diet) this is not only mentally healthy, but physiologically boosts the body's levels of fat-burning hormones. Imagine: a cheat meal that, rather than hindering your fat burning program, instead enhances it.

Do yourself a favor: spend more of your money on high-quality foods. For example, fresh-baked bread from a bakery using quality ingredients is not only healthier (assuming you are buying whole grain bread and not pastries) than any garbage you buy at the grocery store, it tastes much better. Go to your local farmers market, where you can buy organic produce at better prices than the grocery stores, and load up on fruits and vegetables. What you pay now will save you money in the long run. According to Michael Pollan, in 1960 Americans spent 17.5 percent of their income on food and 5.2 percent on health care. Now, Americans are spending 9.9% on food and 16% on health care. See the connection? Making better, worry-free food choices not only saves you money in the long run but also increases the quality of your life.

On a (somewhat) funny related note, one reason it costs more to fly these days is not the rising in fuel costs. Nope, it's because the average person weighs ten pounds more than before! If you want to decrease your travel costs, do your part and lose the weight, but before you complain about the fat person seated on the plane next to you, keep in mind an airplane doesn't distinguish between fat and muscle, so those of us who've packed on muscle mass over the years aren't helping the cause either. Oh well, you can't have it all, all of the time.

Do check out Michael Pollan's book, In Defense Of Food: An Eater's Manifesto, it's an excellent read.

ARE YOU PREPARED TO ACTUALLY TAKE ADVICE?

Advice is a funny thing: some people love being in the advice-receiving stage. They just can't get enough advice. No matter how much great advice they receive, they always feel they need more before even thinking about acting on any of it. Rather than following good advice and achieving their goals, they've made the act of receiving advice their goal. Not a bad idea when writing a book on the advice, but even if that's your goal, at some point you'll still have to trade in your advice-recipient hat for an action-taker hat.

Then there are people who hate receiving advice: they think they know it all and don't want any advice from anyone. They never seek advice and if they happen to receive it, they never follow it. As a result, their growth is hampered and at some point, usually comes to a screeching halt. You can only get so far with what you know: in order to go from where you are to where you want to be, you need to learn more and act more.

Another category involves people who only seek advice, which is in line with what they currently believe. In other words, they're looking for validation when they request advice, not objective advice. These advice/validation-seekers have only their illusion of open-mindedness in reality they just want people to agree with them. They've made validation-seeking their goal rather than a genuine impetus for growth. You're only going to learn so much from people who tell you what you want to hear and share your same views.

Let's back up a bit and take a closer look at the advice-receiving addicts: why do they love being in the advice-receiving stage? When we receive great advice we get excited about the potential of putting it into action. Thinking that the advice may help us achieve our goals is exciting; however, at some point you have to go from the anticipation/excitement stage to the action stage. And once you start thinking about putting the advice into action, reality kicks in and you realize that following through on the advice is harder than remaining in the advice-receiving stage. People receive great advice all the time, yet few actually do anything with that advice. For the advice-receiving addict, the remedy will always be to seek more advice and delay action. The problem with this mentality is you can postpone your entire life remaining in advice-receiving mode. You must take action with the advice you've been given before going back and filling your cup again.

Advice-receiving addicts are frequently addicted to receiving the same advice multiple times. Think of a friend who's called you for advice, received your advice, felt great about that advice...only to call you again an hour later asking for the same advice. This cycle goes on for years if you're not careful. Advice-receiving addicts like having problems - whether they know it or not because it makes them feel important. When you receive advice, especially from people you admire, you're receiving their attention along with their advice, and this can be addictive. If you follow the advice, solving the problem, you no longer merit the attention. Advice-receiving addicts are unconscious of this motive, desiring to assure the continuing advice/attention fix over releasing their addiction by putting the advice they've received into action.

Next, let's look at the people who hate receiving advice: they tend to be pretty miserable people. If you think you know it all, how can life be exciting? After all, one of the greatest joys in life is interacting with - and learning from - those interesting people who can profoundly affect your life. People who hate receiving advice are usually in repeat mode, wherein every year is the same - for years on end. Ten years go by and nothing significant has happened since the same year has repeated ten times over. The advice-haters may be action-addicts who are simply too busy making their endless moves to stop and benefit from any useful advice but, unfortunately for them, their personal growth, and enjoyment of life, plateaus or even declines because they've failed to slow down and reflect. An action-addict's action is a distraction device, just as advice merely distracts the advice-receiving addict. If advice-receiving haters were more open-minded, their action would be more efficient.

The funny thing about advice-receiving haters is they love giving advice to others! After all, they've got the know-it-all mentality and feel an ego-boost when others approach them for advice. More often than not, they prefer to disburse advice they themselves wouldn't follow and the advice they give others is often negative: they're the people who'll tell you why your goals and dreams won't work out rather than offering constructive advice. Just as they can't take good advice, neither can they give it.

Now let's take a closer look at the final category, which are the advice/validation-seekers: advice/ validation-seekers only want advice, which aligns with what they already believe. For example, an advice/validation seeker may have a problem with his business, but while the problem lies within his business structure, or even himself, he wants to believe it's an external factor. Rather than seeking sound and balanced advice, the advice/validation seeker is looking for someone who's on his same page. His motto is: I only accept advice that's in line with what I already believe. These people hold the illusion that they're open to advice and even benefiting from advice but upon closer scrutiny it's clear they're merely seeking validation. Because advice/validation-seekers aren't receptive to the possibility that they're in error, they never grow beyond their own egos. They simply follow their own advice, and when they doubt that, they look for external validation.

Advice/validation-seekers simply don't want to change and grow: they want to justify their homeostasis.

How do you know which category you're in, if any? By using the example of a fitness trainee: if you spend more time researching training programs and emailing fitness professionals for advice than actually training, you're addicted to receiving advice. You enjoy getting attention/advice and, for you, pursuing training advice is your goal over any training results. If you're o.k. with that, keep it up; just don't hold any illusion of actually get stronger, losing fat or whatever your training goal is by chasing advice. At some point, you must leave the comfort zone of the advice-recipient and become an action-taker. Don't shed any tears since there are plenty of opportunities to get more advice after you've taken a few critical action steps. As a bonus, with your new, real-world experience, any new advice will hold more meaning.

Continuing with the fitness trainee example: if you're someone who's been on the same program for ten years and haven't made any training progress since the 1990's, it's time to finally take some advice and resume your long-lost progress. Thinking you're too good for advice, you've made an illusion of self-reliance your goal. Think again: be open to advice so you can get back on the path of personal progress.

Still using the example of a fitness trainee: if you ask a fitness professional for a solid training program, then continue using the ineffective program you were already on, you're not seeking meaningful advice, only validation. Of course, that's fine if that's your goal. But if you actually desire training progress and you've hit a plateau, it's time to seek advice or do your independent research. As the saying goes: taking the same course and expecting different results is insanity.

While the above categories contain their flaws, they each have distinct merits: There will always be times in which we need to be advice-recipients - being open to advice and gathering as much information as possible before taking action decreases the likelihood of failure. Of course, there will be times in which remaining open to advice isn't the way to go - we need to stay focused while in the action phase and stay the course rather than making mid-course corrections every two seconds. Sometimes, we know what we need to do and seeking more advice only serves as a delay tactic. Finally, there's nothing wrong with receiving validation, we need feedback to know we're on the right track and it's always nice to get the validation of others. Honest validation can serve as a signpost indicating the right direction - just make sure that validation isn't your destination.

In conclusion, get the advice you need, put it into action, and enjoy the validation that comes with being on track. Be honest with yourself and open to reality and you're all set. No need to be addicted to hearing the same advice over and over again and never using it. Moreover no need to be someone that is a "know it all" and not capable of taking advice. Be honest with what you need and have the courage to apply advice that is useful.

BEING ATTACHED TO
RESULTS IS HOLDING YOU BACK

You have a right to your actions, but never to the results of your actions.
Act for the action's sake

— *Bhagavad Gita*

This is a great line that has followed me for many years. It is from the sacred Hindu scripture the Bhagavad Gita, which means song of God. It is considered by many to be one of the most important books ever. This is something I agree with wholeheartedly. It is loaded with an incredible amount of wisdom and every time I read it, I pick up something new. While I have read it many times I never really understood the line above on action until I lived it a few times.

What exactly does it mean to act for action's sake? I am sure it is open to a variety of interpretations and I do not pretend to have the definitive answer. That said, I think it is about fully embracing the present and not worrying about the future. Often we are so focused on where we want to go that we fail to embrace where we are. Goals while very important can also be the ultimate distraction and also make it impossible to enjoy the present. Instead of enjoying what we have during the present, we are focused on some time in what we hope will become our future. Ironically when people get to the imagined "better" time they reminisce on how things used to be.

Of course the past is often embellished, and many of our memories are often close to fabrications to say the least. Thus it is all too easy to get stuck on the wheel of past and future and never be in the present. Sometimes that is a good thing as I do not care to be in the present when getting my teeth cleaned. I gladly put my mind somewhere else and drift away until it is over. What about being stuck on a ten-hour flight? Watching movies on my laptop and listening to music on my ipod is a lifesaver and makes the boring and often uncomfortable trip fly by. Of course when you're stuck next to someone that smells like he has not taken a shower for a week and just ate at Taco Hell then there is not much you can do to distract yourself from the moment. It is going to be a long flight my friend! But I digress.

Nevertheless, when it comes to important actions we want to be in the present. Moreover, when it comes to a career we want to find something that excites us and makes it easier to embrace the present. When I worked in business development in the Internet world, I was often bored out of my mind. The work did not excite me and I found it difficult to be in the moment. I would often look at the clock and time always seemed to go way too slow.

I think a lot of people can relate to monotonous unfulfilling jobs. Some people say that you should embrace the job anyway and be present regardless of whether you find it exciting or not. They say you will be happier being present then playing the distraction game. Perhaps, there is some truth to that but I think it is better to have an honest internal dialogue and instead choose another path. If you are dissatisfied it is time to find something that is satisfying. Comedian Billy Gardell says if you're an adult and on antidepressants you need to get another job! I am sure there are many cases of chemical imbalances that cause depression and medications can be useful in such cases. However, I think the majority of people that are de-pressed need to take charge of their lives and make some serious changes rather than take medications to alleviate symptoms.

Usually the gratifying path is right in front of you but you are too busy distracting yourself and listening to advice from others to see it. It also helps if you are not texting all day, wasting time on twitter, or watching moronic reality TV shows.

Mike Mahler

If you ponder on it for a while, I'm sure you have had positive experiences in which you were fully in the present. Most likely it occurred without you thinking about it and that is what it is all about. Back in undergrad I experienced this when I got into religious studies. I was just not into college until I found some courses that engaged me.

Once I found an area of strong interest I went from just passing classes to being on the dean's list. The dean's list was a side effect of really enjoying what I was studying rather than being the actual goal. I could care less about grades and working hard to get an A on a piece of paper was never a motivator for me. In addition to doing all of my course work, I used to go beyond it and read even more about the topics I was studying.

Trust me you're not going to spend your free time reading and researching more in college unless you are really into the topic. Most students do exactly what they need to do to get whatever grade they are going after and no more. I did not do the additional work for a pat on the back or extra credit, I did it because I genuinely enjoyed it and wanted to immerse myself in it fully. I was experiencing first hand embracing my actions fully without being attached to the results of my actions. Ironically, while I was living it, I was not conscious of it and did not make the connection at the time. I did learn one very important thing and that is I only do well at things I genuinely enjoy. More importantly I get depressed when not occupying my time with things I enjoy doing. I have learned that this is a blessing in disguise over the years.

Most people are very practical in college and instead focus on what they feel will get them a high paying job after college. Again the focus is on what they will be doing after college rather than what they are doing in college. A very common example of failing to focus on actions and instead being overly attached to the results of actions.

It is much harder to focus on an area of study that genuinely interests you, as you are sure to get a lot of push back from people around you. Whenever I told people that I was majoring in Religious

Studies, people would often respond in an incredulous manner. In their minds the only path I could take with a religious studies degree was to become a college professor. I knew at that time that I had no desire to be a college professor. However, I also knew that I was never going to make it through four years of college focusing on something that I could care less about. Somehow I knew that things would work out and there was no point wasting time worrying about it.

Funny thing about college is when you graduate everything you learn seems to stay there. The real world has a way of slapping you in the face hard and it is back to reality. Religious studies gave me a philosophy for life, but it was not necessarily what I wanted to do career wise. What I knew I wanted to do was right in front of my face and that was something fitness related. I did not put enough energy into a direct path and just did not see a clear route at the time. I did not want to be a trainer in the gym and to my myopic mind at that time, training in a gym seemed like the only option. Thus, I decided to do what I failed to do in college and that is to be practical. Have you ever gone to a ton of job interviews for well paying jobs that you could care less about? It is boring at times but often comical as well. The generic questions that you are inundated with are always amusing. Where do you see yourself in five years? My mental response was hopefully not here. What value will you bring to our office? My mental response was probably not much as this job looks boring as sin but the salary looks pretty good.

Despite my imaginary efforts otherwise, somehow I managed to get hired. Keeping the job on the other hand proved to be much harder. Either I would reach a tipping point and quit or my employer would reach a tipping point and fire me. Paradoxically I often got fired after bringing in a lot of business for the companies. After getting fired a few times I finally got the message. I think companies just know an entrepreneur when they see one and perhaps people that take charge and make things happen are just not a good fit for many companies. I am half joking of course but one thing was for sure, there was no way I could focus on my actions instead of the results of my actions while doing something that did not excite me. As long as I worked for others in jobs I could care less about I would be like a lot of people in the workforce who live for weekends and vacations. I have even heard people talk about the rest of their life in terms of weekend and vacation time. Now that is just flat out depressing. While I respect anyone that has a job and works hard and in the recession we are in I can see why many are happy to have a job, I have l always needed more. I need to actually enjoy what I am doing.

A good friend of mine had been telling me for many years that I am a natural entrepreneur and that I should do my own thing in the fitness world. I used to spend a lot of my free time reading training books and discussing training with others. It was time to make my vacation my vocation and to quit playing the distraction game and make it happen. This is something my grandfather did. He realized that working for others was not a fit for him at all. He had a personality in which he could not stand working for others and employers could not stand having him work for them. He went on to build a very successful consulting company. While he made good money, that was never his focus. In fact he often undercharged, as the juice for him was the actual process. He loved what he did and would have done it for free. The money came from focusing fully on his actions rather then the results of his actions.

When I finally pulled the trigger and jumped full force into the fitness world I knew it was the right move. That feeling of excitement that I had in college was back and that feeling is priceless. You cannot buy it or fake having it. You wake up every day excited about what you are doing and have the freedom to move in different directions in order to keep things exciting.

I started my fitness business with a focus on kettlebell training. I took a great course with top strength coach Pavel Tsatsouline and knew right away that kettlebells would be a big hit down the road. I loved training with them and it gave me a unique selling point as no one at the time was trying to build a kettlebell-focused business. My friend and fitness expert Steve Maxwell was teaching kettlebell classes at his gym but kettlebell training was not his primary focus.

I liked the business model of workshops and wanted to focus on that avenue. I also did other things that were fitness related that I enjoyed such as writing articles for magazines and websites, teaching classes, private lessons, online consulting etc. However, the primary focus was on doing workshops and lots of them. I liked being in front of a positive group. I remember my very first kettlebell seminar like it was yesterday. It was in Northern Virginia back in 2002. I trained eight people in a park for a few hours and made five hundred bucks. I was on cloud nine. I was just so happy to be doing something I enjoyed and actually making money doing it. I was living in the moment, enjoying my actions and was not worrying about the results of my actions.

I moved out to Los Angeles in 2002 for a change of scenery and to build my business. I wanted to be where all the action was. Los Angeles is often called the city of dreams but it can also be a city of nightmares. I have never been to a city with so many broken down people. People that had dreams when they moved to LA but for whatever reason failed to have any success. I did not want to fall into that category and wanted to persevere in Los Angeles.

I put the pedal to the metal and worked my tail off. Every day I woke up ready to crush it. I was making things happen but unfortunately despite my efforts I ended up with more month than money! I played the credit card shuffle game to keep things going but it was not enough. The debt was piling up and in addition I was in a relationship with an energy vampire, which certainly did not help. If you are planning to move to Los Angeles and are trying to decide if you should move alone or with an energy vampire, pick the former. Trust me I have been there!

If you have heard any of my hormone optimization lectures you know I emphasize the importance of addressing financial and relationship stress. These are often the two largest stresses that we deal with and having both at the same time is not much fun.

What started off as a fun adventure was quickly turning into another job. Instead of focusing on the actions and enjoying the process I was now focused on how to make money and lots of it. Again, making money should be a side effect of the actions not as the primary focus. I had learned that lesson twice but needed to learn it one more time to really comprehend it.

The result of the financial and relationship stress landed me in the throws of a life threatening case of pneumonia. Both of my lungs were filled up with bacteria and I nearly died from it. I lost thirty pounds during the illness and when I looked at my bank account I only had $7.00 left. It was time for a paradigm shift. It was time to rebuild and do things right. Eradicate the personal life stress and get back to having fun again. Enjoy the process and get committed. Six months later I was making a livable income. While it was certainly not a lucrative income it was enough to pay the bills and keep my head above water. A year later I was making a very good income and a year after that I was making a great income (income is all relative but by my standards it was a great income and that is what matters). I was making more than I ever made working for others! The best part is the money was not the focus. I was focused on making the business fun again and getting back to why I got into it in the first place.

I have kept the fitness business fun and fresh by going into other areas of interest. While my fitness business started as a kettlebell focused endeavor it has evolved into much more. I have managed to integrate much of my life philosophy into what I do via my online magazine. In addition, I have managed to stumble on another ground floor opportunity via conveying hormone optimization information. It is a topic I am excited about and one that others cannot get enough off.

This is how you live in the moment and enjoy your actions. You find something that you find exciting, have the courage to pursue it, and also keep evolving. Many trainers and people in general tend to accumulate a certain amount of knowledge and then keep repeating it over and over again instead of evolving. Knowledge can be a trap as well if you have the illusion that you have enough of it.

Making money is of course important and I would be lying if I said that it is not an important focus in my business. However, it is not the focus but a side effect of enjoying the process and finding ways to keep the process enjoyable. There is no excuse for letting things become flat and boring. When you carve your own path you can always find ways to keep things engaging. That is the beauty of doing your own thing.

There is a disappointing trend in the fitness world now in which many trainers care more about marketing information than training information. No doubt, marketing information is critical and I spend a good amount of time learning about marketing. It is one of the key ingredients that I used to build a successful business. However, when you look at every potential client with dollar signs and decide that actually training yourself is no longer a good use of your energy you are in the wrong business to say the least. How are you supposed to get others excited about training when you never train or train in a lackluster manner? When I talk to my peers such as Jason Dolby, Ken Blackburn, Steve Cotter, Jon Hinds, and Steve Maxwell they all have one important thing in common: they love training! They love doing it, they love talking about it, and they love teaching it to others. This is one of the main reasons why all of these guys are successful. Not just financially but successful in living fully. When you meet these guys in person you realize they are all genuinely happy.

It is not the end of the world if you no longer enjoy training and teaching it to others. It is just a sign that you need to move on to something else. What should you do? That is for you to decide but there is always barber college if nothing else comes to mind!

There is nothing wrong with enjoying the results of your actions. I don't think there is anything wrong with going on expensive vacations, buying big houses, fancy cars etc. But those can all be fun side effects of working hard on a labor of love. However, I think you miss out on something very important when that is what you are all about. That "thing" is the presence of the moment, the full enjoyment of your actions without the worry of the results of your actions. All worrying ever does is increase your stress hormone levels and make it impossible to enjoy the moment. Focus on the now, the later will be there waiting for you when you get there.

Goals are important, as you want a target in which direction to go. However, don't be so attached to your goals that you are blinded from the present. Goals are often anti-climatic because our expectations on what achieving goals will do for our happiness is inflated. We often fail to realize it when it is happening, but the real reward and fun is in the action not the results of the action.

While many feel grateful to have a job in the tough recession we are in and others would love to have any job, I still think it is worth asking more of ourselves and striving for something more fulfilling. When you do something that is gratifying it is much easier to live in the moment and being able to fully embrace the moment is priceless as it is the noteworthy experiences that we accumulate that make our lives rich.

In conclusion, do you have a right to the results of your actions? Yes you do but the results will be much better if you focus fully on being great in the action phase without being distracted by the results of the action phase. Moreover, the action phase is where the visceral living is and where the fun is as well.

DOING WHAT YOU LOVE IS HARD WORK

Many people have the illusion that people who are passionate about their line of work are happy campers that have found Nirvana. They just look so happy when they are working and boy, it must be nice to be full of joy all day long. They forget that one of the definitions of passion is to suffer for what you love. People that love what they do, do not settle for mediocrity or doing a pretty good job. People that love what they do want to be great at it and to be great at what you love you have to suffer. It becomes an obsession that is on your mind all the time. You are always thinking of ways to improve. Trust me you work much harder when you do what you love then you ever do just doing a mundane job.

While the brutal reality is that you will suffer in order to be great at what you love, the key point that distinguishes it from doing a mundane job just to get by; is that it is the kind of work that you actually want to do. This is a critical distinction as work that you actually want to do is gratifying and fulfilling. The kind of work that you do just to get by may pay the bills, however, it is never gratifying or fulfilling. Now I am not knocking anyone that works. You do what you have to do in life to survive and I have respect for anyone that is willing to work hard to make an honest living rather than be a vampire living off the misguided generosity of others. However, the fact remains the same. If you do not love what you do, you suffer twice. You suffer while you do it and you suffer from the lack of fulfillment. If you do what you love, you only suffer once. You suffer when you put in the necessary concerted work to be great but have the incredible sense of fulfillment that only doing what you love for a living can provide.

Author Malcolm Gladwell in the book Outliers states that it takes ten thousand hours of concerted effort to reach a level of mastery in any field. This is not ten thousand hours of playing around. No, ten thousand hours of focused energy on your craft. This level of focused work is very difficult and few have the discipline and the pain tolerance to push through day after day. It is all too easy to make a processed meal in the microwave and watch four hours of mind numbing reality TV instead. Ten thousand hours of very hard work and sacrifice is what separates the exceptional from the mediocre. Now if you do not love what you do then it is highly unlikely that you are going to put in ten thousand hours of concerted effort. You probably will not even be willing to put in half that number. No matter how much you want the goal, if you are not prepared to endure the process you can forget about it. Of course if you are not prepared to endure the process then you never really wanted the goal to begin with.

The ironic thing is the process of being mediocre at something is often fun. This is what I like to call the hobby stage. When you are in the hobby stage nothing serious is at stake. It is a hobby and not how you make your living. There is no real pressure to be good at a hobby. Hobbies are fun and a nice refuge from the various stresses that come with living. However, when you decide to turn a hobby into a full-blown vocation a total flip-flop occurs. Now the pressure is on and it is no longer refuge from hard work and stress - instead it becomes hard work and stress! Yet once again it is hard work and stress that you choose. It is hard work and stress that you want to take on and that is what makes it a powerfully life changing process.

When you have a big smile on your face at all times and get giddy about pursuing a goal then you are still in the amateur phase. It is easy to get excited about what you are doing when you have only been doing it for a few months. It is easy to get excited about what you are doing when you do it as a part time gig and make your real living doing another job. It is much harder to push through when a hobby becomes your sole way of making a living. Now it is no longer something you do when you feel up to it. No, now it is often something you do when it is the last thing you want to do.

I am friends with a few professional comedians. If you did not know better you would think that comedians are happy-go-lucky people. However, the opposite is often true. Many professional comedians actually have melancholy personalities such as the ones I am friends with. This is hard to believe when you see them up on stage acting funny and making people laugh. Nevertheless, think about what comedy really is. It is either an expression of self-deprecation or humor at the expense of others. It is taking things that that ranges from negative to depressing and repackaging them in a way that makes people laugh.

To come up with hilarious pieces comedians have to go into dark places often and spend a lot of time there. Then they have to work their tails off traveling all over the place doing gig after gig of the same material. Whether they are up to it or not is relevant. They have to do a great job or forget about having a great career. Is it fun? Sometimes it probably is. A lot of the time it probably ranges from not so fun to downright miserable. Sounds terrible right? Wrong once again it is work that they want to do. Being a successful comedian is arguably one of the hardest jobs around and no one is going to take it on as a career unless it is something that they are passionate about. I have no doubt that pulling off a great gig is gratifying and fulfilling, but I doubt that it is always fun. In fact in my own way I know it is not always fun. It is time for another personal story to illustrate these points further.

I first started teaching kettlebell training workshops back in May of 2002. My very first workshop was at a park in Northern Virginia with a whopping eight people that paid around $65.00 to attend the course. That fee is around six times less than what I charged at my last workshop in 2008. While the money was not great back then (although it is not bad either for a days work) I had more fun at that workshop than at any workshop I have done since. I was so happy to be in front of people teaching something that I really cared about. Up until then I had always done jobs just to make money. These jobs were never enjoyable and certainly never fulfilling no matter how much I got paid. My very first kettlebell workshop on the other hand was both enjoyable and very fulfilling. I had a great time, the group had a great time, and I even met one of my best friends at the course Dylan Thomas who went on to become a great kettlebell instructor. Talk about a day well spent!

I went on to do a lot of kettlebell workshops all over the US and even one in the U.K. Every time I did a course I got better at teaching. I also got much better at promoting the courses and putting together more professional productions. What do I mean by professional production? Partially, it means that the courses actually took place inside a nice facility as opposed to a park in Ohio in the middle of winter (something that I actually did). As the courses became better something else also happened. They became less fun. How is this possible? I am better at teaching the courses, I am using much nicer facilities, I am getting more people to attend, I am making more money than ever, and at the same time the courses are not as fun. What happened? Somewhere along the way I went from being an amateur pie in the sky instructor to being a serious professional.

It takes a lot of work to put on a great workshop and the teaching part is not the hard part. The hard part is promoting a workshop successfully and making sure the entire production is organized and fluid. If you want to teach a course to a few people in a park whenever the feeling strikes that is one thing. You can keep that fun and casual. However, when you want to take it to a much higher level it becomes a lot of hard work and lets face it hard work is not fun. Sure working hard and pulling off great events is fulfilling and gratifying but that does not mean it is fun.

What is interesting is that as the courses became less fun, they also became much more fulfilling and gratifying. As the workshops became less fun, my confidence went up. When I first started doing kettlebell workshops I used to have a detailed outline that I studied the night before. Now I could walk into the room without any preparation and do a bang up job. Also, just because I did not feel like doing a workshop for whatever reason did not affect my performance at all. If I felt excited about doing a workshop, I did a great job. If I felt like crap and did not feel like doing the course, I still did a great job. In fact some of my best workshops were ones in which circumstances were far from ideal.

One of the best workshops I ever put on was a course in NYC back in 2004 in which everything that could have gone wrong went wrong. The students came into the course ranging from irritated to angry and if I did not bring my best game it was game over. In fact it could have ended my fitness career. That is how dire it was. I certainly was not excited about teaching the course. Regardless, my assistant instructor Dylan Thomas and I brought our best games and turned the whole disaster around. People came in irritated and angry and left happy and on cloud nine. Many of us got together for dinner after the course and everyone left dinner with a big smile on their faces. We also met one of the best strength coaches around at the event Zach Even-esh. Talk about non-fun day that was well spent!

The entire process was very hard work, but it was by far one of the most gratifying courses that I ever did. Was it fun? No it is not fun having to turn angry people around but man is it gratifying.

A few years ago I put on a big production workshop that was even less fun and yet very gratifying. Some of you were there and many of you have the DVD set of the actual course. Yes I am talking about the Collision Course Workshop.

Collision Course was a departure from the usual kettlebell workshop that I had done over the years. Instead of having a kettlebell focused course I decided to make kettlebells part of the overall pie rather than the entire pie. Collision Course featured a section on Battling Rope Training with Guinness book record holder John Brookfield. The course had an incredible section on the benefits of strongman training taught by legendary strongman competitor and expert strength coach Mark Philippi. Jon Hinds of the Monkey Bar Gym taught an outstanding very high-level section on bodyweight training. I taught a section on hormone optimization and also advanced kettlebell training. I also had two guest presenters at the course that did a bang up job: Tom Furman on joint mobility and Dylan Thomas on kettlebells for the martial arts.

To make the offering even better for the attendees, I hired my brother Roger to film the course to turn into a DVD set. Everyone who attended the course received a copy of the DVD set for free. It was a great course that really only had one problem, which unfortunately was not enough attendees! I lost thousands of dollars on the front end and had to pay many of the instructors out of pocket.

My inside joke about the course is that the attendees paid a lot of money to attend but no one paid as much as I did to be there. While it was a great course it was not profitable. I did everything right to make the course successful financially. It just did not pan out that way. Yes I could have cancelled the course but I do not like doing that. This is a course that I believed in strongly and I did not want to disappoint the people that paid to attend. Sure I could have paid the instructors less but I gave them my word on what they were going to get paid and I wasn't about to look for the easy way out at the cost of my reputation. Instead, I decided to take the risk of doing the course and make my money back on the DVD set.

Now many amateurs would have cancelled the course. If they actually put the course through they would have done a minimalist job. After all this was not a course that did not make much money it was a course that lost money! I actually made more money at my very first workshop in Northern VA. Not exactly the way I wanted to come around full circle. It is hard to have fun when you work your tail off and lose money. However, it is not about having fun when you are a professional. It is about doing a great job irrespective of the circumstances. It is not the students fault that the course was not profitable and I wasn't about to disappoint them.

To make a long story short, people loved the course. This is obvious if you watch the students on the DVD set. They are having a blast and the feedback was overwhelmingly positive. Honestly, I did not have fun at the course. There were too many things for me to be accountable for in addition to actually teaching at the course. The fact that I lost thousands of dollars to do the course did not help either. Nevertheless it was gratifying to put together a unique course that the attendees really enjoyed. Moreover, it was very fulfilling to put out a great DVD set of the course. Not only did I make all the money that I lost back I was able to put out a unique offering that people really enjoyed.

No doubt you have to love what you do in order to be great at it. Perhaps not always the actual process but the gratification and fulfillment that comes from being a professional and doing a great job. If you work your tail off and do not receive strong sense of gratification and fulfillment then it is clear that you are not doing what you love. It is time to be honest and do what is necessary to find something else when you can. Moreover the amateur stage is only fun for so long. At some point you have to become a professional to keep growing as a person even if it means the fun is over. Fortunately fun has nothing on gratification and fulfillment.

YOUR FLAWED DECISION
MAKING PROCESS IS WHY YOU FAIL

Its not easy for the brain to choose a long-term gain over an immediate reward – such a decision takes cognitive effort – which is why getting rid of anything that makes the choice harder is so important.
— *Jonah Lehrer, author of* How We Decide

Every January people start yet another year excited about achieving their latest goals, hoping this is the year that they finally make things happen. Yet tragically, most people give up on their goals before January is even over.

Why do people fail to see their goals through? Do they simply lack discipline and perseverance? Are most people so delusional they don't care about achieving the goals they've set? While we could argue both those points, according to Jonah Lehrer, author of How We Decide there's still more to it and it starts with our brains, specifically those parts of the brain which affect the decision making process: the emotional and rational brains.

It's important to take the time to determine how it is you make decisions. Does the emotional brain persuade you? Or does the rational brain dominate? What are the pros and cons of the emotional brain and the rational brain? More importantly, is your current decision making process (or lack thereof) holding you back?

Let's start by taking a look at the pitfalls of being emotional-brain dominant. The emotional brain seeks immediate gratification and seeks to avoid that which it perceives as pain and loss. Further,

84

in attempting to make sense of things (that may have no real explanation) the emotional brain looks for (non-existent) patterns. Yes, in some ways the emotional brain is delusional.

The immediate gratification aspect of the emotional brain make credit cards and your emotional brain a disastrous combination. When using credit cards to make purchases, the brain doesn't cognize any sense of loss. When pulling cash from your wallet, the eyes see - and the fingers feel - your wallet immediately lighten. In this way, through the sense organs, the rational brain will kick in to supervise cash purchases. However, with credit cards, the rational brain often fails to show up - why is this? The eyes see something the mind desires and if no impending loss is factored in with an exchange of cash. Before you've consulted your rational aspect, the transaction is done by credit card. The emotional brain loves shiny credit cards and without the rational brain to balance out this unhealthy affection, you could find yourself in big trouble. That the average U.S. citizen carries over $10,000 in credit card debt is a perfect illustration of what I'm talking about.

Most of us can relate to the experience of receiving a credit card statement and feeling shock and disbelief at the balance. We wonder how did all of the charges get there? The first reaction may be to wonder if your credit card was stolen! Then, as you carefully peruse each itemized purchase, reality takes a seat beside you. In fact, you did buy all those things and the total is correct. Promising yourself to never repeat this grievous mistake and wishing to celebrate your new found discipline, you take your credit card to the local bar and buy everyone a round! Yes, the emotional brain is easily seduced by that temptress, the credit card. To the emotional brain, credit cards offer the illusion of both immediate gratification and pain avoidance when, in fact, it is merely immediate gratification. Going into consumer debt, with its high interest rate, is the epitome of pain and suffering, thus, paradoxically the long-term loss inherent to credit card debt is the very thing the emotional brain is so desperate to avoid.

Poor food choices are another example of the emotional brain in action. Since the long-term negative consequences of wrong diet take time to manifest, the emotional brain hones in on the immediate gratifications of junk food. If consuming fast foods resulted in instant heart attacks or visibly expanded guts or - bam!! - cellulite, then it'd be easy to refuse. Unfortunately, the damage accrues slowly - compounding over time much like consumer debt. Similarly but with a different outcome, the positive effects of appropriate exercise and sound nutrition also take time to accrue - which is one reason why people find it difficult to stay the course. If people could join a gym and eat a few good meals, instantly gaining muscle and losing buckets of fat from a little proper nutrition and exercise, well, it would be easy to keep it up! Unfortunately for the undisciplined, the diligence of training and dieting is generally too much to ask of the modern person operating from the emotional brain. The entire process is instead (mistakenly) perceived as an (undesirable) loss. In this endeavor, we must harness the rational brain to help us see the truth behind the appearances. In this way, using both aspects of the mind, we can eventually meet our physical goals and the emotional brain can bask in the gratification of looking and feeling great. Without hitching up the rational brain, however, few of us are able to endure the discomfort, which is all too obvious when you look around you and see the current vogue of obesity.

Investing is another area fraught with disaster when dominated by the emotional brain. The emotional brain's fear of loss causes it to miss the big picture ironically creating more loss. According to Lehrer, statistics show that from 1926 to the present, stocks have always outperformed bonds with an average annual return of 6.4% versus 0.5% for bonds. Nevertheless, in an attempt to avoid risk many investors place most of their savings in bonds, and end up losing significant potential earnings in the long run. If people enlisted their rational brains in their decision making process, they might realize that index funds (such as Vanguard's total stock market fund) are safer, more lucrative, choices, especially for younger people with a longer time span before retirement. For those investors closer to retirement age, bonds can be a sound choice.

Another ambiguous brain terrain is your career. Emotional brain-dominant people often work - for other people - in jobs for which they have no passion, since the emotional brain, desiring to avoid (perceived) loss at all costs, will resist the risks of pursuing your dream occupation. "Risk aversion" is the excuse people make for remaining in hateful jobs while postponing their true vocations. Yet the current economic crisis clearly proves that job security is as big an illusion as ever existed. The reality? You're better off recognizing what it is you want to do for a living, then creating a plan (and putting in the necessary effort) to get there. However, first you'll need to win over the emotional brain and its inherent reluctance to take risks and avoid perceived loss...that or do hard time in a miserable job. It all depends on your definition of "loss".

After reading this much about of the emotional brain, you might think the rational brain to be superior. Not so fast! Before attempting to relinquish all emotion and become a real life Mr. Spock, let's take a closer look at the shortcomings of the rational brain. According to Lehrer, relying too much on the rational brain leads to over analysis, which results in inaction. In addition, the rational brain can cause you to over value information, i.e. sensory input, if not balanced with the intuitive cognition of the emotional brain. Finally, while the rational brain loves information, it can only handle so much at a time. Too much information creates a state of over stimulation, which leaves the mind distracted and confused, thus understanding little. Rational brain-dominance retards your overall growth potential.

Any time you learn a new skill the rational brain comes into play. Remember when you first learned to drive a car? Everything was new so your rational/conscious brain broke the skills down move by move: fastening the seat belt; shifting into drive; and pressing the foot to the accelerator pedal. Over time, as you acquired the skill of driving and the task shifted to the emotional brain, the rational brain played a less significant role. In short, once you know what to do, you needn't consciously think about it. (On the other hand, given the skill set of the typical Las Vegas driver, most would do well taking a step back and letting their rational brains do the driving - perhaps they never brought them out in the first place!)

To recap: learning a new skill is the domain of the rational brain but once you've assimilated that skill, the emotional brain retains the memory. This is efficient since the rational brain can only process a limited amount of information at a time. Once the skill is acquired, the rational brain empties its cup to the emotional brain to better analyze new incoming information, leading to new skills. If you continually function from the rational brain, your thinking pathways will quickly become rife with clutter. It's the sleek emotional brain that operates without the clumsy burden of conscious thought, thus the rational brain can purge its tendency to excess baggage.

Still, there's a hitch: you must consciously choose to enlist the counsel of both the rational and emotional brains. Otherwise, it's too easy to favor the one while avoiding the other. Engaging the rational brain to learn a skill, then assigning the memory to the archival emotional brain requires letting go of the conscious thought process - which is easier for some than others. But hoarding skills in the rational brain is the source of pedantry, among other character flaws. Attachment to the rational brain (or the emotional brain - or anything else! - for that matter) is a habit, a form of comfort. If it's an entrenched habit, even life long, learning to re-wire the brain for better balance will take time and conscious effort. The good news is you can use the rational brain to acquire some new, intuitive/ emotional skills! It all starts with learning more about your true self and understanding how your mind functions. Not an easy task but truly the most important task of your lifetime.

You see, while the rational brain is great at researching and analyzing information, it is not very good at distilling emotional truths, i.e., assessing what it is you really want. If you're continually amassing and scanning information, your emotional brain is blocked from doing what it does best, that is, discerning truth from appearances. This is why over analysis is simply another form of distraction - what I call active procrastination. As long as you continue to research and analyze, you preclude the emotional brain from making any decisions, and in this way, you'll never see any action. In fact, this is how to delay action indefinitely, since action is defined by the possibility of failure. As long as you fail to act, you'll never have to worry about failing out in the world - or so the rational mind would have you believe. Of course, you'll fail to pursue your goal, but somehow this detail gets overlooked in the analysis of the externals.

Too much information is like too much food, you choke and go into a panic. The key is to choose your sources of information wisely, using discernment. The rational brain is like a valued servant, blocking the mind's entrance from street riff raff. Use the rational brain to acquire the appropriate information in the right amount of information, then take some time off from data processing to make any relevant decisions. Genuine wisdom requires both aspects of the brain.

For example, let's say you wish to decide whether to quit your job in order to pursue something more meaningful. First, using the rational brain, consider the pros and cons, once you've done a thoughtful analysis, allow yourself some time to digest your thoughts. The emotional brain, through the process of discernment, can then assimilate that which is in your best interests, discarding any, well, rationalizations! Thus the rational brain assays the options while the intuition of the emotional brain extracts the essence, collaborating in a wise decision.

Over reliance on the rational brain equates to over reliance on dubious information, i.e. sensory input, and can result in poor performance. To illustrate this point, Lehrer references a study from Stanford University wherein the study subjects consumed an energy drink prior to completing a test. Group A paid full price for the drink while Group B was offered a significant discount for the same drink. The full price group outperformed the discount group. It seems that Group B assumed their discount drink was inferior and so their performance suffered. This is a case of the rational brain drawing a conclusion from a arbitrary price, which is simply information. Assuming you get what you pay for can have a shadow side, since that which costs more money isn't always superior to that which costs less. It can be complicated, which is why we need our archived, intuitive/emotional intelligence. It is neither adequate nor wise to solely rely upon sensory information via the rational brain.

In order to make good decisions, we need to be well-informed, but too much information (or even too much information access) can be overwhelming. This brings to mind the typical person I encounter within the fitness world. Most people have neither the patience nor discipline to adhere to a single program long enough to derive its maximum benefit. For example, one week they'll commit to training for a kettlebell sport competition, then they read an article about Clubbell training and switch tactics. The following week, a new magazine comes out with a feature article on Strongman training and our trainee becomes excited. Then it's all Strongman training for a week or so until they read about the benefits of sandbag training...you see where this is going?

Sometimes the best move a trainee can make is to assess his goals and choose a program, then avoid doing any further research for the duration of that program. Follow the program from start to finish with no modifications or rationalizations. Then re-assess and do some more research. This is harder then it may sound! In our information glutted society, with myriad free programs on the Internet, plus books and magazines fitness and training, it's no wonder people have difficulty picking one program and persisting, since choosing one program entails a sense of loss over all the other programs out there. Let the rational brain assess your goals and resources, then access the emotional brain's cognition of the appropriate course of action. Intellect is a powerful tool, but an imbalance of intellect can narrow your field of vision.

So at this point, it sounds like the rational brain and emotional brain are both flawed. Perhaps they are, in their lower, undeveloped natures - as are we all. The best we can do is to continually refine our rational and emotional processes so that we're functioning at a high level of cognition. This requires a balancing of both the rational and emotional brains, what amounts to a friendly dialogue between the two. In this way, the emotional and rational brains regulate each other. We need ready access to both aspects in order to make our best decisions. We can regulate a hyper-emotional response by pausing and allowing the rational brain to, step in and assess any situation. On the other hand we can regulate rational thinking by cutting off analysis before it goes into overload, cutting off further sensory input, and appealing to the emotional brain for guidance.

The emotional brain informs you of what it is your heart wants while the rational brain puts together your best plan for acquiring it. After you've done the requisite research with the rational brain, it's time to take a break and let the emotional brain and its intuitive aspect come up with an original idea. When you are tempted by impulse purchases, give the rational brain some airtime and initiate an internal discourse. The rational brain can help you delay gratifications and even help you see the merit in making present sacrifices for future rewards. On the other hand, the emotional brain will help you live in the moment instead of always awaiting a future that never arrives. Of course it's all about balance: too much delayed gratification detracts from the joy of the present moment while too little delayed gratification prevents putting necessary plans in place for the future. In order to live life fully, we need to master the best aspects of both the rational and emotional aspects of ourselves.

Too many people live their lives on autopilot, never understanding why they feel so much agitation and dissatisfaction. Taking time to think about who you are,and how you make decisions, is very important to your overall well being. Failure to achieve your goals is usually due to your own flawed decision-making processes. Take the time to observe whether you are emotional brain dominant or rational brain dominant. What effect has this had on your life? Don't just assume things will simply get better with time, time is fleeting. Instead, learn more about yourself and how your mind works and make things better now.

ADDICTION TO CONSTANT ENTERTAINMENT MAKES SUCCESS IMPOSSIBLE

We're an entertainment-addicted society. We need to be entertained at every waking moment and who knows, maybe even our dreams are next. Four hours of TV per night is no longer enough: we need to be able to watch TV on our cell phones, have TV monitors in elevators to be entertained on the fifteen-second ride to our floor, and even in cabs - heaven forbid we look out the window and observe the world as we cross town. We even view thought-provoking video commercials while standing in line at the grocery store - the possibility of boredom while waiting to buy things is unacceptable!

Restaurants now have TV's positioned around the dining rooms so every guest can enjoy the pleasure of moronic television shows and avoid talking to the people in front of them. Thanks to cell phones, we enjoy eavesdropping on intellectually stimulating conversations of strangers around us as they get input from friends and family on important decisions such as whether they ought to get Cocoa Puffs or Fruit Loops at the grocery store. Forget using cell phones for emergencies, use them all day long and exploit as many meaningless conversations as your plan allows!

It's a good thing we have computers and the Internet at work: faking working has gotten so much easier this way. You no longer have to be bored at work, i.e., actually doing your job, now you can spend the workday day on idiotic message boards talking to people that you'll never meet in real life. When that gets boring, you can spend the rest of the day watching home video clips on YouTube. Once another "productive" day at work closes, it's time to go home and spend the evening entertaining yourself further with such stimulating TV shows as The Real World and Keeping Up With The Kardashians.

No need to think about what you'd actually want to do with your life nor what line of work you'd enjoy. Work isn't supposed to be fun and a job is supposed to be, well, a job! That's the bill of goods you've bought - hook, line and sinker - and why shouldn't you follow the masses? Just keep distracting yourself with entertainment outlets, and when you're on your deathbed you won't have the regret of inadequate entertainment during your fulfilling lifetime.

It seems many movie and TV production companies are all-to-aware of our addiction to entertainment and her fat cousin, spectacle. Thus they no longer bore us with neither complex plots nor dialogue in movies and shows. Why bother with character or story development when we can watch things blowing up and otherwise getting tossed around for ninety minutes? Ah yes, it's fun being part of the MTV generation! Forget about movies which might inspire people to live more fully. Nah! Living vicariously is the in-thing, and the masses are skilled at it. In fact, if the sport of living vicariously through entertainment ever becomes an Olympic event, we'll win, hands down!

You'd think that with our addiction to entertainment and our access to information we'd no longer accept boring jobs, only doing what genuinely interests. Yet that's not the case. Many people accept a bill of goods that jobs are boring and you'll have to put up with forty-plus hours of boredom per week, then get in as much entertainment as possible during off-hours and weekends to make up for it. Hell, if you can get in as much entertainment as possible when you're at work, via the Internet, who says you can't have it all?

Unfortunately, our entertainment-addiction hasn't carried over to the places where it really matters. It's used instead as a coping mechanism to accept our lives as they are without bothering to change. After all, why bother taking risks and doing the hard work that it takes to make the changes necessary to living a fulfilling life? Far easier is vicarious living through others, via entertainment sources. But entertainment rarely inspires us to make our own lives better, merely substituting for deeper experiences of life. When we disassociate the entertainment from our experience of living, we don't see the obvious connection of how one, when used properly, can improve the other.

In addition to being an entertainment-addicted society, we're also a society which no longer understands the concept of delayed gratification. After all, not having what we want - right now - is boring! Working hard and sacrificing are unacceptable options; we want things now and if we can't afford those things, there are friendly, and generous companies willing to lend us the money it takes to make all our material dreams come true.

These lenders, of course, have our best interests in mind, only charging a reasonable 20% plus APR to borrow money, so we can buy the mountains of things that we need to fill up our garages. Want a big screen TV but can't afford it? No problem! Just sign up for the monthly installment plan and spend the rest of your life paying it off. Who cares if the $4000 TV ultimately costs you $20,000 in interest fees, when - and if - you ever pay it off? You must live fully in the moment and refuse to sacrifice the now! After all, that's the secret to enjoying life, right? If you cannot afford something, get it anyway and worry not about the consequences - maybe you'll get lucky and die, sparing yourself the worry about paying back the money.

A result of our entertainment addiction and hatred of delayed gratification, is that saving money is now an outdated concept. Money is for spending, in order to be entertained now. Putting away money is boring and doesn't at all support our present entertainment. As for the future, I'm sure things will just work out fine--right? I hope so.

It's no wonder that moronic sayings, such as fake it until you make it, are so popular today. Our society has become very good at faking it: we fake liking jobs we hate; we fake enjoying lives that we detest; we fake being happy when we're miserable inside. We fake being who we aren't and yes, we even fake financial wealth when we're living month to month. Well, you can't fake success or happiness, no matter how hard you try, so don't bother. Further, if you work hard, and pay the price of success, you'll never have to "fake it". If you do some self-reflection, and determine what makes you happy, you don't have to fake it.

I don't think there's anything wrong with watching TV or a good movie. In fact, while 99% of TV is garbage, the few quality shows are better than all the campy shows that used to be on many years ago. Spartacus, Lights Out, and Breaking Bad are all well-made shows, with good acting and engaging plots. Shows like these, in addition to being engaging, can actually provoke independent thought. Addiction to entertainment, and using it as a substitute for living a genuine life, is a slippery slope for some, and an avalanche for most. People are better than that and should expect more of themselves.

So where do we go from here? One, stop playing the distraction game. Stop distracting yourself from living your life fully and try spending an hour alone with your thoughts each day. This means no music, TV, reading, no conversations - nothing for that hour. Don't worry, you can go back to your four hours of TV after the hour is up! You may find this painfully boring, which says a lot about your lack of imagination. The more dialogues you have with yourself, the better you'll know yourself, giving you the impetus to make some changes in your life. A more aggressive approach is to unplug the TV for an entire week, turn off the cell phone except for emergencies, and check email just once per day. You'll learn a lot about yourself in a week of unplugging...and you may not like what you find. Brutal reality may be unpleasant but clarity is necessary for growth. Otherwise, keep distracting yourself as the years go by and changes occur, though, most likely, they won't be the changes you want.

ARE YOU A RESEARCH ADDICT OR AN ACTION ADDICT?

While I'm a strong believer in the importance of taking massive action, massive action without adequate research will lead to disastrous consequences. However, choosing to stay in never-ending research mode will get you nowhere fast. Yes, research and analysis are required for any successful plan, but no amount of research will make up for a lack of action: at some point, you have to execute your plan and simply learn as you go.

Repeat: even massive action won't make up for inadequate research and planning (a hard lesson I've learned well) as discussed in previously. You have to act with purpose and a clear idea of what you're doing and where you're going - acting for the sake of acting just won't cut it.

First, lets discuss research addicts. Why do some people resist leaving research mode? For one, anticipation can be more exciting than taking action. In fact, anticipation can be more exciting than achieving goals, since achieving goals can be anti-climactic. Moreover, it's human nature to always want more and never be satisfied; therefore, no matter how many goals you achieve, there'll always be another you think you need to achieve. We can avoid all this by staying in research mode - the ultimate state of anticipation. The more research you do, the more excitement you'll feel in anticipation of (eventually) taking action with all your acquired knowledge. The problem is, you've been in research mode for five years and have yet to put any of that knowledge into action. Oh well, there's always next year.

Second, the more research you do, the more you realize you've a difficult road ahead when you finally do take action. It starts becoming clear that the road may be turbulent and filled with unpleasant surprises. Rather than waking up and facing the world, it's easier going back to sleep and continuing to dream. I call this active procrastination: it's procrastination disguised as something useful, which is the most dangerous form of all. Each time you choose not to act, instead staying in research mode, it becomes that much harder to take action. Yet, you somehow think if you knew just a little bit more, you'd finally be ready to take action. Newsflash: confidence comes from taking action, not from sitting on the sidelines forever.

Third, research mode is safe: as long as you're in research mode you can avoid taking action, and possibly failing. You'll avoid failure and the accompanying ridicule if you avoid taking action. I don't think anyone is afraid of failing per se; no, it's ridicule people fear so much. Just about everyone has bombed-out at something-or-other in front of people at some point and the resultant ridicule has been deeply buried in our subconscious minds, resurrecting itself whenever we go after a goal.

Now, lets talk about the action addicts. Action addicts are people who can't stand research, rather they thrive on constant motion. They don't even care if they get good results, since the stimulus of action is their juice. As long as they're in action, they're able to stay in distraction mode. Action addicts are impulsive people who rarely think things through: they get an idea, act on it right away, and hope it works out. Action addicts are those strength trainees who always want to do more. When they don't get results from training six times a week, they'll start training twice a day. They always assume that more action and work is the answer; the idea of doing less and getting more is ludicrous to them. Action addicts often drink several cups of coffee each day, since you need to get energy somewhere when you're only sleeping four hours a night.

What's the appeal of being an action addict? One, you don't have time to worry about failure if you're too busy acting. You're too busy taking acting to consider failing, even if you've nothing to show for your action. Just because you're taking action doesn't mean your desired results will follow; however, you won't care about that if the action is enough juice for you - who cares about goals! Two, taking action gives one a rush: it's intoxicating and feels like you're in control and moving forward. This feeling is mostly illusory; however, when you're too busy taking action you'll never pause long enough to even notice.

Ironically, action addicts and research addicts generally end up with an equal lack of results. Both are stuck in stimulus mode, neither pursuing the actual goal nor the most efficient path to the goal. Research addicts overload themselves with too much information and have no clue where to go, while action addicts overload themselves with action-for-the-sake-of-action, eventually to burn out. You can only take so much action, without measurable results to keep you motivated.

What should you do if you're one of the above? Try taking a vacation from yourself: if you're an action addict, take a week off and do some research. No action, no reading one paragraph and then going back to action-stimulus mode. If you're a research addict: it's time to put the book down and jump in the water. Start taking some action, since more research is contraindicated.

Essentially, the path to success is a balance between intense research and massive action. Start off with intense research, once you've acquired enough information to get going, then get going with some massive action. Once you've used up all the knowledge, it's time to go back to research mode and load up again. Unfortunately, few people do this. Many simply acquire enough knowledge to get going, never to learn again. Others keep attending seminars, reading books, and doing every other form of research, never to put what they've learned into action. We tend to do what's comfortable rather than what's necessary.

Do what's necessary - and do it sooner than later.

SECTION TWO:
THE IMPORTANCE OF
TAKING SELF INVENTORY

Do You Have the Courage To Evolve?

You have to test yourself everyday gentleman. Once you stop testing yourself you get slow and when that happens they kill ya
— From the movie Young Guns

My favorite books to read are autobiographies and biographies. I also enjoy the Biography channel and watch it often. I love learning about how people evolved over the course of their lives. How they dealt with setbacks, disappointments, and actions they are not proud of. I enjoy the idea that we do not have to settle in life and can evolve and become more. Just because you have done something does not mean you have to keep doing it. You can choose another path. Just because all of your friends hate their jobs and drown their miseries in heavy alcohol consumption every weekend does not mean you have to. They say that life is short; however, if you lead a life of quiet desperation it is anything but short. I think we all owe it to ourselves and anyone that has ever had a positive influence on us to have the courage to follow our bliss. Failing to do so leads to self-destructive resentment and the consequences are often disastrous to not only the individual but to the group.

Making dramatic changes or even seemingly insignificant changes in your life is often difficult. There are many casualties on the road to evolution. Regardless, if you fail to evolve you fail to grow and experience life fully, and what you lose is everything. I hate it when someone responds to the question what is new with "nothing" or "same ole, same ole." It is such a tragic way to live life. Alternatively I always enjoy talking to people that are constantly growing and making things happen. Their enthusiasm and accomplishments get me excited and I take that excitement back to my life and channel it.

There is no reason why you should not have something new going on all of the time. The clock is ticking and you do not have unlimited time to get everything done. The world is not going to slow down just for you. When it passes you by it is gone and you don't get a redo.

Let's cover five reasons why people fail to evolve and then get into some examples of people that had the courage to go in a new direction and grow.

First, many people fail to evolve due to self-destructive addictive personalities. Relying on will power to change is a battle of attrition and you will always lose that battle. Once energy is created it cannot be destroyed only transformed into something else. Thus instead of trying to quit an addiction, it is more effective to accept you have an addictive personality and change the focus. For example, instead of being addicted to junk food with no nutritional value whatsoever become addicted to being fit, strong, and healthy. Trade the high of junk food for the high of feeling great everyday by supercharging your health and vitality.

How about instead of being addicted to complaining about your life and the shortcomings of others you get addicted to helping others? Studies show that we derive the most pleasure from helping other beings. When you occupy your time and energy with productive actions it is no longer a battle of attrition. The focus has changed. Your energy has been re-directed. You're not spending your energy resisting something; you're spending it doing something else all together.

In the first Matrix movie (yes the only good one) the character Morpheus tells the reluctant savior of humanity Neo that when he accepts his calling he will no longer have to dodge bullets. Relying on will power is similar to trying to dodge bullets all day long. Eventually one will hit you and derail your plans. It is only a matter of time. However, once you change your focus and find a new path to put all of your energy into, impressive change is possible.

Second, another reason why people fail to evolve is they spend too much time talking about personal traumas and not enough time taking empowering actions. Moreover, many people spend too much time complaining about what I like to call luxury problems failing to realize that they're lucky that their problems are not more severe. We are not going to waste any time covering how people should get over luxury problems. Instead we shall focus on how to move past real traumas resolutely.

In her excellent book *Lifting Depression*, Kelly Lambert PhD explains why talk therapy is often ineffective in prevailing over trauma. Lambert states, "Contrary to popular belief, talking about the traumas of your life may not help you to move from depression to mental health. In fact in some cases this approach may impede your natural path to resilience and recovery." When you talk about personal traumas over and over again you relive the experience each time. While getting things off your chest is important eventually you have to live your life and move on. Constantly talking about the same trauma over and over again makes this unattainable.

Often when you talk about traumas, people feel sorry for you and this attention can easily become a crutch. The attention you get from talking about your traumas to others can make you feel important, now instead of getting over it, reliving the trauma becomes the new misguided focus. Often when you unload your problems on someone else there is an energy exchange. They listen to what you have to say and make you feel better but now they feel drained.

Problem talking addicts tend to be real energy vampires and their narcotic is the attention they get from others. Their problems are what make them feel good and whatever makes you feel good is hard to give up.

Talking to friends and experts about things we have been through can be an important release but at some point it becomes a broken record and eventually you need to take that broken record and throw it out the window like a Frisbee. Get it off your chest, get over it, and move on. Burn the bridges of your past traumas and push forward with full force.

Focusing on empowering proactive actions is an effective way to get over negative experiences. The people that ultimately overcome abuses are the ones that find a way to use their harsh experiences to help others.

Third, people often fail to evolve because their perception of life whether conscious or unconscious is too comfortable. Daniel Coyle in his outstanding book *The Talent Code* quotes psychologist John Bargh to drive this point home, "If we're in a nice, easy, pleasant environment, we naturally shut off effort. Why work? But if people get the signal that it's rough, they get motivated now." I can definitely relate to what Bargh is saying. When I first started my training business I was barley getting by. Making money to pay rent and keep my head above water was on my mind constantly. I worked seven days a week and was never really comfortable. Even when I tried to relax it was always in the back of my head. What was I going to do today to push my business forward? How was I going to make it this month? These were questions that were constantly on my mind. As my business grew and more money came in, just getting by was no longer a motivation. I was getting by just fine and had to focus on other things to keep pushing forward.

When we moved from Los Angeles to Las Vegas the upgrade in lifestyle was tremendous. We moved from a small apartment to a spacious house. Talk about a comfort zone literally! When I am not on the road, I am working from home and it is all too easy to avoid getting things done; if you lack discipline. In addition, my business has been well established for several years and I am fortunate to have a nice income even with the tough economy we are in. This is yet another comfort zone and it is all too easy to just unwind.

While I think down time and relaxation are critical components of life, it is definitely possible to get too much of both. In order to stay out of the comfort zone I take risks every year. No I am not talking about moronic risks such as putting my life savings on a poker chip at the Las Vegas Strip. I am talking about calculated risks such as investing a good chunk of change into new products and projects. I also spend a great deal of time learning about new things to keep my business evolving and relevant. It works and it keeps me sharp and on the edge where I need to be to keep evolving.

Doing the same thing over and over again is a sure fire way to go out of business. Companies that do not evolve die and while the same is not necessarily true for people, I think people's spirits die when they fail to evolve. Evolving requires taking risks and taking risks is very important to keep life exhilarating.

An interesting side note is that the one positive of our down economy is it has given some people the impetus to pursue careers that they have always wanted to do. Many people are getting laid off and realizing that there really is no security in working for others. Thus, it makes sense to find something that is exciting and have the courage to pursue it. I know several people that have decided to become entrepreneurs after getting laid off and last I checked many of them are doing pretty well. I am not just talking about income either. I am talking about being excited about life, which is an important marker of success that is often overlooked and not taught.

The flipside of comfort zones is it is easy to make the uncomfortable comfortable. All you have to do is gradually lower your standards and accept less and less until you're unrecognizable. This is how many people get obese. It does not happen overnight, or in a week or month, it happens gradually over several years. The same thing occurs with regards to credit card debt. Just pile up a few expenses here and there over the course of several years and now you have massive credit card debt.

What it comes down to is this, the best way to lead a gratifying life is to be thankful but also to be dissatisfied. Not dissatisfied like some ingrate that complains all day long about luxury problems, but dissatisfied with your present state of development. The most interesting people I know are the ones that are always evolving due to being discontented. Imagine watching a movie in which there is no change in any of the characters at all? Sounds about as exciting as building an ant farm. The best movies and shows always have strong characters that evolve as the story goes along. The most interesting lives are the same way. If you don't focus on making evolution occur then you are just repeating the same year over and over again. Just because ten years goes by does not mean that anything meaningful will occur.

Fourth, many people fail to evolve as they don't value opportunities. They have an attitude of entitlement and when you think the world owes you something you are setting yourself up for serious stagnation. In *The Talent Code,* author Daniel Coyle details an interesting story that supports this fact.

Coyle writes about a violin program that was put in place in the inner city. One school had great success with it and the other school failed miserably. Both schools had the same demographics and even the same teacher. Why did one school reign supreme over the other? The successful school initiated a lottery program. Only the kids that won the lottery were able to join the program. The other school allowed anyone to join. The kids that had to go through the lottery system were excited they won and treated the opportunity with more value. The kids at the other school did not value the opportunity, as the opportunity was not qualified.

Legendary strongman competitor and top strength coach Mark Philippi uses the qualifying method to help high school kids at his training facility. Mark is a generous guy and wants to help kids who cannot afford his services. What they learn from Mark often makes the difference in earning an athletic scholarship. However, he is not a chump and is not going to waste his time working with lazy ingrates who expect something for nothing. Thus, Mark makes a deal with potential prospects. He offers to train them for free in exchange for work at his training center. The students have to mop the floors, clean the toilets, and do any other job that Mark needs completed at the training center. Not surprisingly, many kids say forget it and walk out the door. However, the ones that are serious jump at the opportunity. To them it is a no brainer. They get free training from one of the best strength coaches in the country and all they have to do is some labor in exchange. These young men and women come ready to work hard and get the most out of Mark's expertise.

When you do not value an opportunity it is all too easy to miss out tremendously. You only get so many opportunities in this life. Those that evolve are well aware of this and when they are presented with an opportunity they pounce on it and never let go.

Fifth, some of our beliefs often prevent us from evolving. Our beliefs can be similar to material things that we're overly possessive of. Just as hoarders have an onerous time relinquishing material possessions, many people are hoarders when it comes to their belief systems. Even when the truth slaps them straight in the face, they choose not to see it and take comfort in being unyielding.

Not being open to new ideas reminds me of an old Buddhist story. A man in a small village got word that his son died in battle. He mourned the loss of his son and then eventually moved on with his life. Several years later the son returns home. Apparently he did not die in battle. He knocks on his father's door but the father refuses to open the door. He is convinced that someone is playing a cruel prank and is attached to the notion that his son is dead. Even when his son is knocking on the door he refuses to be open to the possibility that he is alive.

Many people hear the above story and just roll their eyes. After all who would be that obtuse? They of course miss the entire point of the story, which is to convey that our preconceived beliefs often prevent us from seeing the truth, even when the truth is right in front of us. While being too open-minded makes one a target for exploitation, not being open-minded makes you a self-induced mark for never evolving.

We often define ourselves by what we believe, and to surrender it is to give up our entire being. After all what are we without our dogma? While change is often frightening, a more important question is: What do we miss becoming, by failing to relinquish dogmas that prevent us from growing and enjoying life fully?

Now that I have covered five reasons why people fail to evolve, let us go through two case studies of people that had the courage to evolve, and one that is the master of evolving and staying relevant.

A man that had the courage to change when old dogmas were proven erroneous was the civil rights activist Malcolm X. I studied the life of Malcolm X a great deal when I was in college majoring in religious studies. I was going through some major transformations myself and I found his story fascinating to say the least as he made several serious transformations throughout his all too brief life. Recently, I was reminded of Malcolm's powerful evolutions after reading Jesse Ventura's American Conspiracies.

As a young man Malcolm X was a criminal that hated being black and wanted desperately to be white. He straightened his hair, only dated white women, and wanted to be wealthy and powerful. His criminal life eventually landed him in prison where he was exposed to the teachings of Elijah Muhammad and the religious cult The Nation of Islam (NOI). The NOI teachings infused with Black pride and Black Nationalism had a profound effect on Malcolm and he surrendered his criminal lifestyle and became a devotee. Malcolm was able to quit drugs, alcohol, smoking, and his criminal ways by changing the focus. His new focus was the NOI and empowering his people through its teachings. Malcolm's new focus, natural charisma, and hard work ethic allowed him to grow rapidly in the NOI ranks. Eventually he became the right hand man of Elijah Muhammad.

For several years Malcolm espoused the NOI dogma aggressively. He blamed white people for all of the ills and suffering of African-Americans and pushed for a separate state. Over time Malcolm eventually realized that the NOI had strong elements of corruption that stemmed all the way from the top. He tried to rationalize the corruption he came across but eventually he had to look into it further. Not long thereafter, Malcolm was kicked out of the NOI for making some disparaging remarks about the assassination of President John F Kennedy. Some believe this was just a convenient way to get Malcolm out of the organization before he learned too much. After all he was a highly influential leader and could cause problems for the corrupt members of the organization.

Once out of the NOI, Malcolm spent volumes of time studying traditional Islam and was startled with the incredible discrepancies. For example, unlike the NOI, traditional Islam does not teach that an evil scientist named Yacub made white people. Traditional Islam does not state that any one race is superior to another. The serious discrepancies between the Nation of Islam and traditional Islam became even more apparent to Malcolm after he made a pilgrimage to Mecca in Saudi Arabia. In Mecca, Malcolm met Muslims of all nationalities and races. He had many human rights discussions with Muslims from all over the world and came to the conclusion that no one corners the market on human suffering. It is a global problem that needs to be addressed globally.

Malcolm again had the courage to evolve when the truth slapped him in the face. He could no longer bury his head in the sand and instead went on to embrace traditional Islam and denounce the teachings of Elijah Muhammad and the Nation of Islam. Even when death threats were made against Malcolm and his family he stayed the course. In the book American Conspiracies, Jesse Ventura states that Malcolm had a meeting with Martin Luther King Jr. and that they were planning on collaborating to push civil rights further in the U.S. Tragically both were eventually assassinated before they were able to bring this vision to fruition.

It would have been interesting to see how Malcolm continued to evolve as he got older. While we will never know, there is something we can learn from Malcolm on having the courage to evolve. Just because Malcolm was a criminal as a young man didn't mean that he had to be a criminal for the rest of his life. Just because he was seduced by anger and racism at one time in his life did not mean he had to be a racist for the rest of his life.

He had the courage to evolve as he went through the craziness of the human condition. Many people remember Malcolm for his anger against white people and assume that was all he was about. Imagine for a second that you are judged for the person you were twenty years ago or when you were a teenager. Would you say that is a fair assessment of who you are now? I think it is safe to say that we have all done things in our lives that we're not proud of. While we cannot go back in time and make changes we can choose to evolve now and become something better.

Now let us go to the other end of the spectrum and discuss a highly intelligent lady that has done an incredible job staying relevant for almost three decades. I am talking about the one and only Madonna Louise Ciccone otherwise known as the top selling female recording artist Madonna. Madonna became a pop sensation in the early 1980s. However, there were a lot of pop sensations in the 1980s and very few of them, if any, are relevant in 2010 besides Madonna. Whether you like her music or not and personally I don't, Madonna is clearly a sharp woman that knows how to stay current as the years go by. Her music has evolved over the years and she is not afraid to discuss politics, religion, sex, and spirituality. She could have easily just played it safe and pumped out music with trivial themes year after year. Instead she chose to let her music be an expression of whatever she was going through and people continue to resonate with the authenticity.

Madonna is also an incredible marketer and is not afraid to take risks and plenty of them. When you play it safe and never take risks you will become irrelevant very fast. Madonna is also great at creating controversy to the point that people wonder what she is going to do next. Is she going to go on the Larry King show and talk about the Kabbalah and why her kids have never watched TV? Or is she going to go on the David Letterman show and act like a lunatic? Being unpredictable may be risky for a politician (although it would be refreshing); however for a performer it is an effective way to stay relevant when used advantageously.

Not all of Madonna's risks of course paid off. For example, some of the movies she starred in were pure disasters such as Shanghai Surprise, Evita, and Swept Away. These terrible movies are the kind of films that have the power to end careers. Regardless, if you study any successful person you will realize they have made far more mistakes than successes. For example the only record that NBA legend Michael Jordan holds is for most total misses! While he is remembered for being a great player that made a lot of shots the reality is he missed a lot more shots than he made. This is very common with very successful people. We tend to fixate on their successes and fail to see that they generally have a lot more failures than successes. The difference between successful people and mediocrity is the successful do not dwell on failures. They learn from their failures and push forward.

Many people fail to realize that you're not going to hit a home run every time you're at bat. In professional baseball you are considered an excellent player if you hit the ball three times out of every ten at bats. This means an excellent player is missing the ball seventy percent of the time! Many people give up too easily due to a few or even one mistake. The key is to make mistakes, learn what went wrong, and evolve forward. You do not get good at anything by not making mistakes. We learn much more from our mistakes then from our successes.

Now if you thought that going from discussing Malcolm X to Madonna was a strange transition you are going to fall out of your chair when you read about who is up next.

Forget about other end of the spectrum, it is time to go to another dimension. This one is going to make many of you laugh, as I am laughing right now as I type this. Who am I talking about? Robert Matthew Van Winkle otherwise knows as the rapper Vanilla Ice.

Yes I think it is safe to say that this is the first time in history that Malcolm X, Madonna, and Vanilla Ice have ever been mentioned in the same chapter. You may be thinking that I have lost my mind but bear with me a little bit and see where this is going.

Vanilla Ice was a commercial success in the early 1990s with his signature song "Ice Ice Baby." This song was the first hip hop song to top the Billboard charts. In addition "Ice Ice Baby" just so happens to be one of top kettlebell instructor Ken Blackburn's favorite songs. Ken likes to practice his timed kettlebell set work to "Ice Ice Baby" and "Play That Funky Music."

Now I remember Vanilla Ice's music well as I was in high school when he was popular. I was really into the NYC hardcore scene and heavy metal music at the time and could not stand Vanilla Ice's music. I thought it was the cheesiest stuff around. Vanilla Ice also made what is likely the worst movie in the history of movies Cool as Ice. Talk about taking a risk that back fired like a faulty bazooka!

Soon after his popularity dissipated, Vanilla Ice went into a fit of depression over his career. I cannot say I blame him, as I would be pretty depressed to if I was in the movie Cool as Ice. All joking aside, Vanilla Ice was not proud of the fictitious past that his record label created for him (essentially saying he was a poor white kid from the hood) and the overly commercial music that he was talked into making.

His anger turned inward, and prompted him to attempt to commit suicide. He survived and realized that he needed to make some serious life changes. He had to find a way to make his life more authentic and find an expression outlet that empowered him. He wanted his music to be an accurate representation of how he was feeling rather than some shallow commercial nonsense. With the encouragement of some close friends he decided to shift genres and put out some intense rap-metal music instead of commercial one hit wonders that never stand the test of time.

He went on to make several rap-metal records and while none of them were huge commercial successes the albums represented the kind of music he wanted to make and as a result he developed a loyal following. He played in smaller sized venues all over the country and was much happier with the new direction. I read a few reviews of Vanilla Ice's rap-metal music. Some of them were pretty favorable while others stated that heavy metal must be about to go into a serious decline if Vanilla Ice is getting involved. No doubt going from cheesy commercial hip-hop to intense rap-metal is not an easy transition. However, it is a pretty daring move to make.

Being a fan of rap-metal bands such as Biohazard and Korn, I was curious to check out some of Vanilla Ice's rap-metal music. While I was not blown away by what I heard I have to say that some of it was actually pretty good. It is definitely an evolution in the right direction, which is always inspiring to see.

I think Robert Matthew Van Winkle deserves some praise for having the courage to evolve. It took a lot of courage given the past he has, to try and go into another genre, especially the metal scene, and try to win people over. I am sure most people were not willing to give him the time of day due to his past avatar. Yet he had the stones to carve his own path regardless and I have a lot of respect for that.

Many people aren't proud of things they have done in the past but fail to do anything with it. Instead of pushing forward and evolving and becoming better they fall prey to their mistakes and it ends up defining them. Either that or they attempt to rationalize actions and fail to admit they even made mistakes. If you are not even willing to admit to having made mistakes you will never evolve. Being delusional is a sure fire way to stay in neutral indefinitely. Just because you choose not to see a problem does not mean it doesn't exist.

We all have the power to evolve and reinvent ourselves. We do not have to accept our own self imposed constraints or those that others place on us. We can evolve like Malcolm X, Madonna, and Robert Matthew Van Winkle.

I often hear people say that they're set in their ways and cannot change. It is not that these people cannot change; it boils down to whether you actually want to evolve. We're incredibly adept at rationalizing any behavior and belief system we have. Being delusional comes naturally to people and the consequences are often disastrous to say the least. My studies on why people go evil confirmed this all too clearly.

It is all too easy to say we are meant to be poor because our parents were poor. It is convenient to say we are overweight because we have a genetic predisposition to be overweight. It is simple to say that our fears are a way of telling us that we are supposed to stay put and avoid making any meaningful changes. However easy or convenient it is also a painfully boring way to live life.

In many ways I think life is about facing our fears and pushing through anyway. We do not need courage to act; we need to act in order to be courageous. There will never be a perfect time to act or evolve. There will always be ways to justify not challenging ourselves and taking the safer easier path.

Whenever I am depressed, which I am happy to say is not often; it is because I need to make a change that I am ignoring. There is something that I need to face head on that I am failing to do and I find failing to take charge in life is depressing.

When I push through and face challenges head on I am too busy taking action to be depressed. Taking action is immediately empowering and if you have the right target, one that makes you come alive, you can develop the perseverance necessary to push through setbacks and inertia.

I meet people all the time that complain about their lives, and they all have one thing in common: they spend more time complaining about their inadequacies and no time or trivial amounts of time taking action to improve the quality of their lives. When I tell them how I made changes in my life, they retort by saying that change is easy for me and I am special. Trust me I am not special and change has never been easy. It is always hard.

It is always a challenge to battle inertia and to let go of beliefs and fears that hold us back. It is not a struggle that ever ends, however, what you become through struggling, overcoming, and evolving is the reward and it is a reward worth pursuing.

Do you have the courage to evolve?

THE REAL BATTLE IS WITHIN

Often in life we feel like the world is against us. We constantly battle and compete with others to succeed and persevere. When things do not go our way it is all too easy to blame others instead of taking responsibility. We are becoming a nation of wussified victims in which everyone wants to be part of the club. We take solace in having enemies as that gives us something to focus on and blame. Forget about it being a battle that cannot be won, it is not even the right battle! The most important battle that we will ever face, and one that very few win, is the battle within. We must win the battle within to become self-realized, and we must become self-realized to truly be happy.

There is a great episode of Highlander The Television Series in which the protagonist Duncan McLeod has to battle the evil Zoroastrian God Ahriman. If you are not familiar with the Highlander mythology it is about human beings that are immortal. An immortal cannot die unless his or her head is chopped off. They are drawn to fight other immortals until only one is left. They all carry swords to fight one another and they all agree to a set of combat rules, such as no fighting on holy ground. Yes I realize this sounds like a show created by misfit kids that spent way too much time playing Dungeons and Dragons, but trust me it was a great show.

The series is based on the classic 1986 movie The Highlander, which in my opinion is one of the best movies ever! Ironically one of the worst movies ever made is the atrocious sequel Highlander II: The Quickening. It is one of the few movies I saw in a theatre where everyone watching yelled out "that sucked" at the same time as the credits rolled. The writers of the script for that shameful movie definitely did not win the battle within! Or the battle at the box office as the movie rightfully bombed.

Anyway back to the Ahriman episode. The evil God Ahriman likes to mess with human beings from time to time and is always looking for a challenge. Duncan intrigues him, as Duncan is a fierce warrior that has been alive for over four hundred years. Duncan has always found a way to defeat his opponents and Ahriman wants to break him. Ahriman is very clever, he has the capability to take his opponents strengths, and turn it against them. In his battle against Duncan, he turns Duncan's formidable fighting abilities against him.

He appears to Duncan in the form of previous enemies that Duncan has defeated. Each time Duncan sees Ahriman in the form of one of his previous enemies he attacks with full force to no avail. In fact, each time he strikes out at Ahriman with anger, Duncan becomes weaker and easier to manipulate. The strategies that Duncan used to defeat previous enemies are useless as Ahriman feeds off of one's anger. Anger makes Ahriman stronger and his opponents weaker. As Duncan gets angrier and more frustrated he starts losing his sense of reality and begins experiencing serious hallucinations. During one such hallucination he accidentally kills his close friend and fellow immortal Ritchie.

In a fit of depression Duncan seeks solace in a temple where he remains for over a year. He cannot face what he has done, and does not know how to live with it. Eventually he realizes that he has to stop hiding and face Ahriman. The time for tears and sorrow is over, and the time for retribution is at hand. Duncan returns to face Ahriman but finds that the time away has not improved his strategies against Ahriman. Everything he tries to defeat Ahriman with remains ineffective. Eventually Duncan realizes what was always in front of him, which is his anger. It is Duncan's own anger and rage that has been defeating him all along. Without the anger Ahriman has no power over Duncan. Ahriman comes at Duncan with everything that he thinks will make Duncan angry but this time it is

Ahriman's strategies that are to no avail. Duncan lets go of the anger and as a result Ahriman becomes weaker and is no longer able to attack Duncan. As Ahriman fades away, he screams at Duncan that he is a part of him. Duncan responds that he always was.

Duncan defeated Ahriman by accepting his own evil within. We all have an Ahriman within us, and to deny it only makes it stronger. I discuss this in detail in the chapter on how all people are capable of turning evil. Anger fuels the ego, and our illusory attachment to self-importance. The more important we feel we are, the easier it is to get angry with others. The easier we get angry with others, the harder it becomes to win the battle within and become self realized.

I remember reading somewhere that people who are considered ethical and trustworthy are more likely to take advantage of others after the trust has been attained. The temptation to turn into a scam artist is ironically greater after you have proven to others that you are trustworthy. This is the Ahriman within at work. You get bored of people telling you how great you are and now you want to see what you can get away with. We have seen many popular leaders fall, from having lost this battle within. This process is a gradual one and starts with seemingly insignificant actions, but then eventually spirals out of control until you no longer recognize yourself in the mirror. We are all susceptible to this negative quality and to deny it only makes it more likely to occur. This is why regular self-inventory is critical, as well as surrounding yourself with people that tell you what you need to hear, rather than what you want to hear. We must accept the dualities within us and this is something that every faith emphasizes.

There are many dualities in life. Without having suffered, it is impossible to truly feel pleasure. Without having been weak we cannot know what it really means to be strong. Without having gone through financial hardship it is impossible to really appreciate having financial success.

I know exactly what it is like to be very unhealthy as I nearly died from pneumonia back in 2002. In actuality, I should have died as I flew to Uganda to visit my parents with only a small part of one lung functioning. I could not even talk without coughing and had to pace myself just to walk from one side of the airport to the other. No question I was a fool to let it get to that point but I am glad I went through it. Surviving it gave me a second lease on life, and made me truly value my life. Something I honestly did not value before that incident. Since then I have never taken my health for granted and have actually gone in the opposite direction of wanting to address every factor of being truly healthy. This is what led me to my hormone optimization studies. Something I probably never would have gotten into if it were not for the near death experience. You cannot win the battle within if you are not alive to fight it.

Self-hatred is another facet of the battle within. Moreover, self-hatred is not always obvious and often people hate themselves without even realizing it. The internal anger that results from self-hatred is incredibly destructive. I know all too well how all-consuming anger can be. It makes it impossible to win the battle within and find real happiness.

Growing up like most kids I just wanted to fit in. I spent part of my childhood in Korea, but most of it in Virginia, just outside Washington DC. I went to school with mainly white kids and many of these kids were very racist. If you were not white you were not part of the club. I always thought of myself as white before meeting these kids as I had more of a Western influence growing up than an Eastern one. I was in for a rude awakening. In addition to being picked on for being half Indian, I was often picked on for being a member of races that I have no connection to, such as African Americans. I was often called the N word and other racist terms.

Instead of becoming angry at the kids for being racist, I became angry at myself, for not being fully white like all the other kids. I blamed my Indian heritage for all my inability to fit in, and wanted nothing to do with it. I thought that if I just embraced my white side, all of my problems would dissipate. It never worked, to deny part of oneself is to avoid fully embracing oneself. Without fully embracing oneself, one cannot win the battle within, just as Duncan could not defeat Ahriman until he came to terms with his inner anger. As I got older I became ashamed for being a coward and not sticking up for what I am.

When I got to college I came across Malcolm X's autobiography. The book really resonated with me. Early in his life Malcolm's self hatred and desire to be white was all too familiar to what I felt growing up. In the second phase of his life Malcolm decided to not try to be white anymore, but to hate white people instead. He blamed white people for all of his problems and the anger fueled him and gave him a strong sense of purpose. That sounded good to me. Hating my Indian side did not work so maybe this time around I would hate my white side instead. Of course as anyone knows who has read Malcolm's entire book, Malcolm eventually evolved to a place in which he saw human suffering as a universal problem, rather than as one that one race corners the market on. I chose to ignore that part as I found the anger towards my white side energizing, and I wanted to revel in it.

Fortunately my anger was quelled when I got into religious studies. It became obvious after studying all the great religions that there are great people in every race, and also terrible people in every race; but the good or the bad is not because of their ethnicity. We have to look at people as individuals and not make sweeping generalizations about an entire race based on a few people. It is absurd and unfair to penalize an individual based on the actions of fellow ethnic members.

Our anger towards others often comes from anger that we have towards ourselves. Looking back I never had hatred towards either of my sides, or any race for that matter. I had hatred towards myself. This self-hatred was expressed as anger towards others, but in the end it was self-hatred. Self-hatred is the greatest adversary when it comes to winning the battle within. At some point we have to evolve way past the hate and strive for greatness. We have to become less self absorbed and become part of something much more gratifying.

There is nothing more gratifying than being at peace with oneself, and that only comes through helping other beings.

Anger is an addiction, and like any addiction the only way to overcome it is to trade it for another addiction. Instead of being angry all the time, I traded it in for being compassionate. Not just towards one race but all people, regardless of culture. In addition compassion to animals is important to me and something that plays a crucial role in defining me.

I embraced both of my heritages, as I am both sides: the Indian side and the white side. There are so many great qualities in both sides, and only a fool would choose not to see that. Both are part of me but neither defines me just as no individual is defined by his or her race. We are all much more than whatever race, or races we happen to be born into.

Over the years I have learned that being bi-racial has many benefits. It allows me to understand a greater variety of people, and not belonging to any one race has its advantages as well. I do not have to worry about ethnic pressure, as I do not belong to any one race. Nevertheless I am often mistaken for a variety of races such as African American or Middle Eastern and this allows me to have a greater understanding of those ethnicities. I know what it is like to experience some of the racism that African Americans experience as I have had such racism directed towards me. The ability to empathize with a variety of people is a gift, and it makes it all the more easy to be compassionate to others.

In life there are always going to be opportunities to cop out and take the path of least resistance. To go against what we know is right, just to fit in. However, integrity is not about doing what is easy. It is about taking the path of greatness, which is never easy. The reward is the path itself. The striving for greatness is the way to win the battle within.

We win the battle within by one accepting that the battle actually exists. Instead of blaming others for our circumstances no matter how justified we are in doing so, we focus on what we can do to take charge of our lives, and have greater understanding of ourselves. You will never truly be successful if you fail to win the battle within. You may have the appearance of success to others, but money, fame, and accolades will not fill the emptiness that you feel. Only becoming self-realized through concerted effort is the path to real happiness, and a greater feeling of peace in this world.

WE ARE GREAT AT
KIDDING OURSELVES

A few years ago, Dr. Bruce Nadler (otherwise known as The World's Strongest Plastic Surgeon) committed suicide. Worse, according to forensic analysis, he shot and killed his wife point-blank before going into the next room and killing himself. We hear stories like these all the time, but what makes this one different is I knew the guy: we both spoke at the Fitness Business Summit in 2007. My wife Carol and I chatted with him and his wife and they were very nice people. After my presentation, Dr. Nadler made a point of shaking my hand and telling me how impressed he was. Like most people, I never would have guessed he suffered from depression and that, almost a year later, his depression would reach critical mass, resulting in murder and suicide.

My initial reaction upon learning of Dr. Nadler's suicide was shock, then, when I heard about how he killed his wife, it turned to revulsion. Taking your own life is one thing, but taking someone else out with you is not your right. That he murdered his wife is beyond disturbing.

I've become very interested in the study of happiness over the last years, and thinking about the Nadler murder/suicide my brain's been turning non-stop. I wonder what Dr. Nadler was like at my age? Did he suffer depression then? Did he have any idea he'd go on to commit suicide at the age of 61? Further, when he and his wife married did he have any idea he would murder her many years later? I have no idea and never will, yet, if I had to guess, I doubt Dr.

Nadler held any of those thoughts. My guess is he was happy at my age and enjoyed his married life and being a doctor. Maybe I'm mistaken, but I doubt he was clinically depressed for the last thirty years. So what happened? I have no idea, but it got me thinking: where will I be in my sixties? Will I still enjoy life and continue growing as a person, or will I feel depressed with no desire to live? The latter seems unlikely given my current level of happiness, but none of us really know what lies ahead.

We can spend our time planning out our lives, setting goals and creating an illusion of control over this crazy world, but in reality we have little - if any - control. You can be in the best shape of your life and on cloud nine one minute, then get hit by a car the next, spending the rest of your days as a paraplegic. You never know what's around the corner. Then, every once in a while, we'll predict something that comes to pass, feeding our ego and again reinforcing the illusion we can see our future - yet it is just that: illusion.

The Buddha taught all life is suffering. Sounds depressing from a superficial analysis but the deeper meaning is our suffering is due to attachment. When we lose something to which we feel attachment, it can become the tipping point over an edge. I don't think there's any single reason why Dr. Nadler killed his wife and then himself - I think there was a tipping point as he stood at the edge of his life. It's more likely his final scene was a culmination of several concurrent frustrations.

From the Buddhist point of view, it's not what happens in our life that makes us suffer, but how we interpret it. In one of my favorite books ever, Viktor Frankl's Man's Search For Meaning, Frankl chronicles his time in a Nazi concentration camp, explaining how some people survived while others lost all hope. The people who survived sought out whatever form of happiness was available to them: If their meal was edible, they experienced great happiness; if someone told a funny joke, they enjoyed the pleasure of that moment as long as possible. Even the warmth of the sun gave them joy. They looked for - and discovered - opportunities for gratitude in the least likely scenarios. Even more impressive, the survivors sought out gratifications wherever possible. Helping out their fellow men was critical: to create purpose to make it through their immense suffering. It wasn't enough to focus on individual survival; the survival of others suffering the same horrors became equally important. Bottom line: those holding strong purpose and meaning in their lives were far more likely to survive than those who lost all hope and thus, meaning.

I don't know why Dr. Nadler took his wife's life, then his own, but I think it's safe to say he lost all hope and saw no reason to go on living. When we lack purpose and meaning in our lives, a part of us dies every day, and it's important to understand this early, before purposelessness, like a virus, replicates within our cells, literally taking over our lives.

Never get comfortable and stop growing. Once you do, you begin dying. My grandfather, a successful businessman, was born in a shack in Montana and went on to become a millionaire and highly sought out consultant to Fortune 500 companies. When working, he was happy, but I noticed upon his retirement he wasn't excited about life anymore, though he still had purpose, since my grand-mother had Alzheimer's Disease and was completely dependent upon him. Her care became his new purpose and reason to keep going. When she passed on, he no longer had a reason to live - but not because he had nothing left to offer. His brain was sharp and he could have engaged in any number of creative projects, but he didn't see it that way and passed on a few weeks after my grandmother.I genuinely admired my grandfather, he taught me a lot about life and the importance of doing what you love; however, his final lesson to me was this: when you lack purpose, the brain and spirit despair and you eventually shut down.

My great grandmother was a different story: she outlived every-one in her life and passed on at the age of 101. She survived breast cancer, her husband's death, the deaths of her sisters, and even those of her own children. She was a simple woman and lived in Montana her entire life - much of it lived alone on a ranch in a small town called Arlee. I used to love talking to her - she epitomized tough. What people consider tough today is ludicrous compared to what was tough in her day. I remember one time she was talking about all of her loved ones dying around her. You could tell she felt very sad, however she ended the story by saying we have to go on no matter what. My great grandmother was many things, but the image I hold of her is of a survivor. No matter what happened to her, she persisted in surviving and thriving. The purposes she maintained throughout her life may be things us moderns would think of as mundane, even tedious, yet where there is purpose there is also survival and delight in life. It doesn't matter your achievements, or any fame you might attain, without purpose none of it matters, like it or not.

I'll never see anyone the same again. Meeting Dr. Nadler and his ensuing deterioration has irrevocably changed me. Now, whenever I meet someone new or talk to a friend, I'll always wonder if they're really happy or just struggling to maintain appearances. Whatever the case may be, I hope you know your purpose and are enjoying this life.

THE HIGH PRICE OF OWNERSHIP

Ownership is not limited to material things. It can also apply to points of view. Once we take ownership of an idea--whether it's about politics or sports--what do we do? We love it perhaps more than we should. We prize it more that it is worth. And, most frequently, we have trouble letting go of it because we can't stand the idea of its loss.

— Dan Ariely author of Predictably Irrational

The notion of our ideas and beliefs as things we own is an interesting one and explains why it can be so hard to grow and develop as a human being. Growth requires letting go of that in which we used to so firmly believe. Once we become comfortable within the constructs of what we think we are, it's difficult to let go, even if we don't like the construct! Many people like neither who, nor what, they've become yet find a coincident comfort there since the known is more acceptable to them than the unknown. Dishonest self-assessments always result in stagnant growth, and when you fail to grow, you fail in living life at its fullest which is a serious disservice to yourself.

How much do we miss in life because of our attachments to who we think we are? The attachment to ownership in particular reminds me of a Buddhist story we spoke about earlier in Section Two: The Importance Of Taking Self Inventory under the chapter titled Do You Have The Courage To Evolve? in which it speaks of a father who is told that his son has died in a battle. The father becomes so attached to the thought of his son's death that when his son appears, alive and knocking on the front door, the father refuses to open it, thinking someone must be playing a cruel trick on him.

You may find it unbelievable that a father won't even open the door to see if his son is standing there, but look closer at your own belief systems you're sure to find a few things to which you're very attached. Some people dismiss ideas and opportunities on the spot, out of fear that openness to new ideas and opportunities will irrevocably change them. Yet their fear of change is irrational, since change is going to occur whether we like it or not - sometimes for the better and others for the worse. Avoiding opportunities to grow and reinvent ourselves is disastrous; we have only so many opportunities in life to grow and improve and they should not be taken lightly.

Worse than an over-attachment to the status quo is the illusion we've refined ourselves when in reality the person we assume we used to be is merely lying low and waiting to rise again. Behaving differently, while helpful, doesn't equal fundamental change. It's easy to lie to yourself and rationalize just about anything. Sometimes we don't accept reality - even when it slaps us in the face.

A great example of this is the "glam metal" scene in the 1990's. In the 90's there occurred an explosion of glam metal bands: Poison, Cinderella, and innumerable other acts. These bands took off commercially and went from playing clubs to filling stadiums, selling countless hit records, and otherwise making tons of money. In the late 90's the scene died off with the rise of "grunge" music and bands like Nirvana and Alice in Chains took off. The record labels dropped the glam metal bands like so many toilet seats. A few shrewd record labels stepped in and offered deals much lower than what the glam bands had been used to, but few of the glam bands dealt, since in their minds they were still popular and entitled to more money. They still owned their belief in their rock stardom, even though reality wasn't on their same page. They refused both the low-ball offers and prerogatives to downgrade their lifestyles and the rest of the story writes itself.

Accepting reality doesn't mean we have to settle for where we are right now, but we must be honest with ourselves, a critical component of instilling meaningful change. If you're broke but lie to yourself saying you have financial wealth, you're not changing anything, just deluding yourself and worse, creating an obstacle to true change. If you're fat and unhealthy yet tell yourself you're lean and healthy, you're lying to yourself while impeding positive change. Faking it until you make it doesn't work. Just make it - then there's no need to fake it.

We know we've achieved true change when we take new actions without having to think about them. For example, maybe you're a selfish person who couldn't care less about others, then, after realizing your own selfishness, you decide to change your ways. At first, you must actively think about others and practice being your compassion skills. Then, over time, you find yourself expressing these new qualities without any prior thinking. This is the sign of genuine change.

One of my favorite movies is the western, Unforgiven, starring Clint Eastwood and Morgan Freeman. Clint Eastwood plays William 'Bill' Munny, a retired criminal and cold-blooded killer. Throughout the movie, Munny repeatedly says he's no longer a killer, he's a changed man due to his wife's influence. Munny has himself convinced of this, until his good friend (Freeman) is brutally murdered by the crooked Sheriff Little Bill Dagget (Gene Hackman). Without hesitation, Munny returns to killing mode, not only murdering Little Bill Dagget, but all of the sheriff's cronies as well. As Munny rides out of town, he threatens to kill anyone in the town - along with their families - who might think about coming after him. Like Munny, we may believe we've changed but it's life's circumstances that are our true judge.

Relinquishing ownership of our self-proclaimed defining construct is never easy. It is a necessity if we want to let go of what we think we are and transition instead into what we wish to become. Life is a cycle of destruction and creation.

Detachment from ownership of ideas and beliefs doesn't mean you stand for nothing.

There's nothing wrong with a strong belief system and unwavering moral code. In fact, both are essential qualities or risk becoming a punching bag in the game of life. However, close-mindedness and rigidity impede personal growth and development. When we stop thinking, someone else will do it for us, and I don't have to explain to you how deadly that is.

ELEVEN REASONS WHY
WE MAKE MISTAKES AND
WHY WE KEEP MAKING THEM

To err is human, and that will never change; however, not taking time to understand the underlying reasons mistakes are made and therefore, continuing to err, is simple ignorance. Humans can do better than this, and it all begins with honest self-assessment and self-analysis. Becoming a student of human consciousness - specifically your own - is critical in understanding what motivates erroneous behaviors and how to transcend them.

The book Why We Make Mistakes, by Joseph T. Hallinan, provides an excellent starting point. Hallinan details the reasons people make mistakes and why most never learn from them. For example, people get divorced from one spouse only to remarry someone else of a similar nature, only to get divorced again, etc. This same scenario replays itself in business as people move from one failed business venture to the next, always wondering why they keep missing the target. In the realm of nutrition, people again and again repeat the same weight-loss diets, though they never achieve their long-term goals. These habitual frustrations create a general attitude of apprehension - a malaise - compounded by the tendency to avoid taking action altogether which is also a mistake.

Hallinan's book gives eleven reasons why we make the mistakes we make - then continue repeating these same mistakes. Some of these reasons may seem trivial, while others will resonate more deeply. While you may relate to some - if not all - of the eleven reasons we make mistakes, you'll certainly find them interesting.

Let's get started on why so many of us have bought one-way tickets to the land of mistake and regret, and what we can do to make a mid-course correction.

The first reason for mistakes is taking more responsibility for a mistaken action than for taking no action at all. In other words, if you try to make something positive happen and it backfires, you'll take this badly, which creates - and reinforces - a reluctance to take further action. If instead, you do nothing (and as a result miss out on the same positive opportunity) you won't take this lack of action nearly as badly as the failed pro-action...thus entire lives are lived with negligible growth.

I experienced this myself when my first business venture turned out poorly. I'd worked my tail off for nearly two years without gaining any forward momentum. Worse, I was worse off than I'd started out. By the time the business officially failed, I was thousands of dollars in debt and to financially recover, I had to take a job working for someone else. What I'd wanted more than anything was to make it as an entrepreneur, so having to take a regular job for wages left me feeling bad, and I wondered if the entire experience hadn't been a waste of time. Yet to assume my sincere efforts had amounted to nothing (that is, that this was the end of the story) would only have been pessimistic and myopic--and I am neither.

In the process of trying to create a successful business, I'd developed several useful skill sets, specifically, I saw what I was capable of when I was driven by a strong belief in what I was doing, which manifested in a tireless work ethic. It was at this time I also developed my public speaking skills, which have proven invaluable in my current chosen work. As a result, I was no longer afraid of speaking in front of groups (and actually became damn good at it) and I'd also acquired that elusive skill of effective interpersonal communication.

In spite of these worthwhile gains in both skills and experience, I was extremely reluctant to launch another business. The pain of the previous failure had made a home in my head and it took some time to evict it. In fact, it took becoming completely disgusted with working for others, in a series of meaningless jobs, before I fully committed to my fitness business.

What I learned in the process of my first business failure has paid dividends in the success of my second, current vocation. In the eight years since I started my fitness business, it was cash-flow positive within the first year and three years in I'd realized a fair income, which I've sustained up to the present time.

While the role of devil's advocate can be useful in making important life decisions, conditioned apprehension results in a life lacking those deeper - and thus more meaningful - levels of experience, including the experience of joy. Making a big mistake isn't remedied by never again attempting anything new and original. Taking calculated risks is the price of living fully. Living life on the bench is secure - maybe even injury-proof - but devoid of any dynamism and contact, which is the essence of living life aggressively.

The second reason for most mistakes is giving too much weight to our initial instincts. We're told by teachers and authorities to trust our initial instincts and tend to selectively remember those times when it works in our favor, rather than all those other times our initial instincts miserably failed us. In reality, our initial instincts are mostly erroneous and worse, is our after-the-fact tendency to falsely remember instincts or intuitions that were never there! In other words, once we already know the outcome, we like to think we knew it all along.

According to Hallinan, first instincts are generally wrong, and studies of test takers have shown that people who go back and change their initial answers often achieve higher scores. Many people won't risk changing their initial test answers - even if they're uncertain of the correct answer - because they have a greater fear of actively marking a wrong answer then of missing through their ambivalence, a more passive form of error-by-default in contrast to the former active, willful error. Once again, this demonstrates the difference between mistakes committed by default and clinging to the known, rather than mistakes caused by direct action taken in the effort to do something right.

The third reason we make mistakes stems from our tendency to look back more favorably upon our past actions than they actually merit. Like proud parents, we delight in boasting in how well our younger selves performed certain tasks which may in fact have been average at best.

This reminds me of when I presented a lecture on optimizing hormones at my Collision Course seminar (Las Vegas 2008.) In my memory, I saw myself as intense and riveting as Al Pacino's character in the movie Heat (and if you haven't seen Heat, immediately stop reading this page and go watch it!) Since my brother filmed the seminar, I was able to compare my subjective memory with the objective evidence on video and, to my disappointment, my memory was not calibrated with reality. Not that I did a poor job, it's just that in my own mind at the time, I thought it was exceptional, not just pretty good. According to Hallinan, being well-calibrated is when our self-perception closely matches the objective reality our self. The truth? The mind's version of ourselves is rarely well-calibrated with the self we present to the world. Short of enlisting a personal film crew to witness our personality in action, this can be difficult to face without flinching or self-censor. In your effort to calibrate internal memory with external reality, a more practical alternative to a personal film crew is requesting honest, constructive feedback from trusted sources.

The number four reason we make mistakes can be traced to that cliché so many of have internalized: hindsight is 20/20. In reality, hindsight -like memory - is fantasy-based, thus an inaccurate account of past events. Psychologists call this phenomenon: hindsight bias. This is how it works: Once we already know how events have played out, we tend to change our pre-event memories. I've personally experienced this more times than I care to admit with the most prominent event being the tragedy of Dr. Bruce Nadler as discussed in the previous chapter titled We Are Great At Kidding Ourselves.

In 2007 I spoke at the Fitness Business Summit, where Dr. Nadler was also presenting. I'd read many of his articles and seen him on Howard Stern and was looking forward to meeting him. He seemed like a really nice guy, excited about entering the fitness business with a new personal training studio in Los Angeles. After my presentation on Internet marketing, Bruce made a point of shaking my hand and congratulated me on a superb job. His wife, who seemed very kind, made a point of complimenting my wife, Carol, about me.

Well, fast-forward one year later and Dr. Nadler is making news for murdering his wife and committing suicide. It seems he'd been depressed over losing his medical license, his fitness business wasn't going so well and...certainly there's more to such a desperate act than we'll ever know. Yet, after I heard the story, my memory recalled Dr. Nadler looking depressed at the Summit. I now remembered walking past the table where he was eating lunch and him appearing noticeably miserable. Interestingly, this memory only surfaced after learning of the murder/suicide - in other words, I invented a memory based upon a known outcome. In fact I had no insight before the tragedy, and when the story broke I was just as shocked as everyone else.

The fifth reason we make mistakes? The myth of multi-tasking. You may have heard that in order to be successful you'll need to be good at multi-tasking, well, nothing is further from the truth! Multi-tasking is instead an excellent way of doing several things poorly or worse, a way to completely fail in several efforts at once. Hallinan claims...We never make two conscious decisions at the same time no matter how simple they are. In other words, it's impossible to do multiple, conscious tasks at once and what we're actually doing is jumping back and forth between disparate tasks rather than effectively working tasks simultaneously.

My own experience is that it's virtually impossible for me to write articles if I have Internet access. Going online is a facile distraction when what I really need is absolute focus on my writing. I frequently disconnect the Internet or go to a coffee house, where I can't get Internet access on my laptop. If I don't block myself from the Internet, I'll typically stop every 10 minutes or so to check email, or research something or other on the web. Every time I lose concentration it takes me awhile to refocus and resume writing. I've found it's far more efficient to concentrate an hour or so upon writing, then take a break and check emails, rather than continuously switching back and forth.

When it comes to the unconscious mind, on the other hand, it's quite possible to work multiple tasks at the same time. For example, I can lift weights while listening to music. Lifting weights is a conscious activity, while listening to music (at least in this context) is unconscious. But what if I tried to do my workout, listen to music, and train a client at the same time? At best, I'd get a mediocre workout, and my client as well. I'd risk potential injury, due to lack of attention or even worse, my client could get injured. Far better for both of us if I concentrate on training the client, then training myself.

Another example is something we do every day - driving. We can all drive our cars while listening to music; driving is a conscious activity, while listening to music is unconscious. However, driving a car while talking on a mobile phone is a potential disaster. When you're engaged in phone conversation you're not paying full attention to driving and if something happens on the road requiring an immediate reaction, you're going to miss it. I once saw a guy driving against traffic while talking on a cell phone, and he didn't stop driving the wrong way, even with traffic coming right at him. Cars in the correct lanes (going the opposite direction) had to drive around him to avoid a head-on collision. This insanity continued for several blocks before he finally realized he was on the wrong side of the road. On top of all this, in his delusion that he was right (and everyone else wrong) he'd been honking his horn at the oncoming traffic - so much for multi-tasking! While you may be able to jump back and forth between multiple conscious tasks, you'll neither save yourself time nor be efficient and effective at any of it. Focus on a single conscious task at a time and do it well, then move on to the next task.

The sixth reason we make mistakes is that we're suckers for anchors and marketers are aware of this tendency and exploit it. An anchor is something that sticks in our head, causing us to take a directed action, which typically occurs on an unconscious level. Grocery stores utilize anchors to sell more products, like a 50-cent can of beans will be tagged as 4 for $2.00. While we needn't buy four cans to get the discounted price, we might anyway now that the number four has been anchored in our minds. Another common anchor is placing an artificial restriction on purchase amounts. In this case, a retail store might limit purchases to 10 units per customer and now that the number 10 has been programmed into our minds, we may well end up buying 10 units of whatever it is. Even if we don't buy all 10, we'll probably still buy more than one, which is the whole purpose of such anchors. This is an especially idiotic ploy people fall for everyday, imagine a customer willing to buy 100 units - would the store refuse?

The above retail examples are fairly benign, thus unlikely to dramatically affect your well being; however, if you fall for these trivial anchors, you may also become prey for those higher stakes purchases like a car or house or otherwise be persuaded into actions not in your best interest. The take-home message? Anchors induce personal actions beneath our level of awareness and it's far better to be cognitive of what you do and why.

The seventh reason we make mistakes is that universal ailment, overconfidence, and the more overconfident you are, the bolder your mistakes. Savvy marketers know most people are overconfident, mainly in thinking they are better than average. If you watch fitness infomercials, you'll see compelling testimonials used to persuade and drive sales, but have you noticed they always include a disclaimer that...such results are not typical of the average person? In my naivete, I thought such disclaimers were for liability issues, but liability is the least of it. What marketers know is that people consider themselves better than the "average" person and thus deserve better-than-average results. Exploiting this delusion, by claiming miraculous results are not typical, flips the phrase into a selling point. Now that you can recognize it, you'll see that every weight-loss and fitness product on TV exploits this strategy - perhaps you've manifested some overconfidence and fallen for it yourself.

Another ubiquitous marketing ruse used to exploit our overconfidence is gym memberships. Gym memberships are always cheaper by the year, or other long-term schedule of auto-billing. The most expensive rates are always month-to-month - without a contract - or drop-in fees. This assumes, however, that you actually visit the gym several times a week! If you only work out once a month, you're overpaying big time.

Yet in their deluded certainty of their superior, i.e., above-average status, most people purchase yearly memberships (if not longer) intending to get the best value for their money. Unfortunately, the odds are not in their favor and in fact, commercial gyms financially rely on absentee members, and would overflow their maximum capacity if the majority of paid members actually showed up on a regular basis. Any given gym's preferred members are those who enroll for a year of auto-billing and never return.

Still another ugly example of our overconfidence backfiring on us is the folly of credit cards. Credit card companies lure new members with low introductory interest rates, sometimes as low as zero interest for six months. However, once the introductory period ends, the interest rate skyrockets without notice, sometimes going as high as 29%! Once again, stubbornly believing in their above-average status, people fall for these zero-APR offers, intending to pay their accrued balance before the impending rate hike comes down. Statistics, once again, prove otherwise and the "average" person averages out at $10,000 dollars in consumer debt.

Not many people escape the mistake of overconfidence. Hallinan writes: ...almost everyone is over confident—except for people that are depressed, and they tend to be realists. Hallinan further writes that the bigger the problems we face, the more overconfidence we tend to display, which only gets us in more hot water. What I'm not suggesting is depression as a cure for overconfidence, but some level of humility and honesty needs to be in place for optimal balance and good character. The know-it-all mentality is one of many fast tracks to a bad end.

The eighth reason we make big mistakes? The plague of information overload; I call this pervasive phenomenon research addiction. While you might think acquiring more information is useful and necessary in becoming well-informed, what typically transpires is we become more overconfident than better-researched. The more we research, the more we think we know - which is the entire problem - becoming a closed feedback loop and progressing to analysis-paralysis.

Research addiction-cum-analysis-paralysis happens all the time in the fitness world where people have thousands of programs to choose from, making it difficult to pick one and stay the course. Compounding this problem is that the more you learn about training, the more training you want to do, and the further you remove yourself from results-producing basics. Powerlifting coach, and legend Marty Gallager writes, in The Purposeful Primitive, that as a trainee, it's much harder these day to attain meaningful results due to the overload of training information - that is, specifically the overload of idiotic training information. Marty says people used to stick to the basics if only because they lacked the overwhelming options available today, and people used to focus on mastering a few movements, rather than seeking entertainment from their training and overcomplicating things. As a result, the average trainee of yesteryear actually got much stronger than the average trainee of today.

While research, and other methods acquiring information, are crucial steps to success, when we overdo it we only end up with full cups spilling out their contents everywhere. Better to empty that cup from time to time. You can do this by periodically teaching others that which you've already learned. I spent most of 2009 researching hormone optimization and other fields of interest, and at this point my head is about to explode and I've got to get back out there and share what I know before commencing any more focused research. This is why I've returned to the workshop circuit this year, in addition to writing a torrent of articles about what I've learned; my cup is brimming and I need to share its contents before refilling it.

The ninth reason for our endless mistakes is that bane to creativity, what psychologists call functional fixity. We can become so set in our ways that we don't recognize more efficient and effective methods of getting things done. Because something used to work doesn't mean it's useful forever. For example, the training programs that produced results when I was 22 are not going to work the same, now that I'm 37, and for a multitude of reasons. Neither will the diet I used at 22 produce the same results it did back then. I can choose to adapt and evolve - thus continue to progress - or I can stubbornly adhere to the obsolete path of the past. I've opted to evolve, and you should too. The truth is you are either evolving and improving, or you are stagnating and worsening your situation; maintenance is an illusion.

Evolution is just as important in business as it is in personal life, and record companies are a perfect example. When the free, file-sharing website, Napster first appeared on the scene, the established record companies, rather than adapting to music downloads as the wave of the future, resisted ferociously. Instead of wasting their efforts in trying to suppress Napster and control the market, they could have made a sizable profit absorbing the new trend. Fighting against evolution didn't work (and never has) and most music sold today is by file download, preferred by both artists and consumers. Today, more music artists than ever before are able to make money off of their craft. Since the artists no longer require a record deal with a major label record company in order to establish themselves, bands often give their music away for free on their own websites, in order to build their customer base, making profits on the back end via live shows and merchandise sales, and consumers now pick and choose the songs they actually want, rather than having to purchase full-length, hard-copy recordings.

Whether you prefer things to stay the same or not is irrelevant; change is a constant in life and you can either adapt and benefit or resist it and be left in the dust.

Mistake number ten is that we're unable to predict our own future actions. People think they can mess around in the present and somehow, in the future, they will acquire discipline. This is unlikely. If you habitually eat junk food in your youth, you'll probably continue to do so as you get older. Start smoking at a young age and you'll probably continue for decades. While we may think we're good at predicting who - and what - we'll be in the future, the reality is another story.

This is why I hate questions such as...where do you see yourself in 10 years? I got asked this idiotic question at every job interview I ever had and usually by some fresh-out-of-college HR paper-shuffler. The kind of person who couldn't herself predict what she'd be doing for lunch, much less in in 10-years time. I don't know if I'll be alive in 10 years, so why bother with where I'll be? Ten years ago I'd no idea I'd be living in Las Vegas and enjoying a great living as a fitness professional and I'm sure that ten years from now I'll be doing something - hopefully fulfilling and beneficial to the majority of humankind - I have no way of anticipating today.

Better to focus single-mindedly on what it is you're doing right now. Yes, we need to plan for the future (to have goals) but not at the expense of missing out on the present moment. If you properly attend to the present, the future tends to be more pleasant anyway.

Trying to control the future from the vantage point of the present reminds me of the saying, Want to make God laugh? Tell him your plans... which perfectly illustrates the folly of human control in the universe.

The eleventh and final reason we make mistakes - especially concerning life-changing decisions - is our captivation with the insignificant. As an example, Hallinan uses his own move out to southern California. Every year, thousands of people move to Los Angeles - not least for the great weather - and likely they assume they'll be much happier there.

Having lived in L.A. for four years, I can well relate to his story. In 2002, I moved to L.A. (from the DC area) to build up my fitness business. I chose to settle in Santa Monica, where I was within walking distance of the beach, and every other amenity Santa Monica offers, like movie theaters, supper clubs and abundant restaurants. Several times a week, I'd train at a park overlooking the Pacific. I won't lie - I enjoyed all the perks and took every advantage, yet within a year of moving to L.A. I almost died of pneumonia .

At the time, despite the sunshine, there were multiple stresses hitting me at onc - -the two biggest being financial and relationship. I was launching my new business and, for the first year, struggled just keeping my head above water. Compounding this financial stress was my relationship with a woman who, over time, revealed herself to be an energy-sucking vampire. Of the two stresses, the latter was worse. I am a hard worker; I know how to make money and it was only a matter of time before my business took off.

Vampira, however, was another story (my lack of experience with the force of destructive relationships didn't help) and the affair took a huge toll on my health. This reminds me of Red Webster's best line from that low-brow movie classic, Roadhouse: I got married to an ugly woman. Don't ever do that. It just takes the energy right out of you. She left me, though. Found somebody even uglier than she was. While my vampire was externally attractive, she was ugly on the inside, which she couldn't hide for long.

So, outside every day the weather was sunny and the beach was only blocks away. The energy of Santa Monica excited and invigorated, but nothing compensates for severe relationship stress. I almost died in that paradise of Santa Monica. I'd have been better off shacked up in Ottumwa, Iowa with a loving, kind woman than with my domestic version of L.A.'s finest, the she-vampire.

Fast forward several years later where I'm living in the suburbs of Las Vegas and married to a fantastic woman. The neighborhood is nice, but is it as stimulating as Santa Monica? Not even close. Nor can the weather compare, and the the hellish summers are especially brutal. Was I happier in Santa Monica? Not at all! In fact, the ways that matter, my life is far better. My health has dramatically improved as I've learned how to optimize my hormones naturally. My moods have lifted as I've learned how to handle the mild depression I've borne for many years. The greatest improvement, however, is I've ditched the vampire, and all those who've tried to take her place. I'm with a loving, supportive (not to mention smoking hot) woman, who shares my same values. I've further been blessed with great finances in these times when so many struggle and endure. These, the important areas of my life, are a lock, and nope, I don't care about the weather! I wouldn't in a million years trade my present life for my former life in Santa Monica.

Well, there you have it! Eleven reasons why we make mistakes, and keep making them. What you do with what you've learned is entirely up to you. You can maintain your overconfidence and keep at what you're doing or, using your inherent gift of human will, choose to do better and undertake the appropriate action.

FEAR IS THE ULTIMATE MANIPULATION METHOD

There are many people in the world who have the best of intentions, but ultimately bring more suffering to the world. Why? Because they are looking to change the world from a place of fear rather than love.

— *Hugo W. Elfinstone*
author of Compassionate Honesty

Fear is - by far - the most powerful manipulation technique. It surrounds us, making it difficult to not internalize. We're so used to living in fear that we not only fear failure, we even fear success! As comedian Jerry Seinfeld said: "The fear of success is proof that we're scraping the bottom of the barrel for things to fear." Why are we so comfortable in our fearful state and why do we allow others to use fear to manipulate us? Well, fear is something we're taught at a very young age. We learn to fear getting hurt and taking risks. We learn to fear the consequences of disobeying orders and we learn to fear not getting what we want if we don't follow the rules. Then, if we ever get it, we fear losing what we have. Ultimately, I suspect we're so comfortable with fear because it makes us feel important, i.e., if someone takes the time to provoke our fear, we must matter. It's an illusion, sure, but what else is new? Lying to ourselves is the oldest pastime.

Some quantity of fear may be healthy (even a necessity) for learning and development, but overall, fear prevents us from realizing our full potential and relinquishes too much power to others. Fear makes people irrational, paranoid, and unhealthy, and raises cortisol (the stress hormone) levels through the roof.

Many companies use fear to control their employees. If you don't arrive on time everyday, you have good reason to fear being fired. If you're in sales, you fear losing your job if you fail to hit your goal every month. Yet any company using fear as a primary motivator inevitably builds an organization of snitches willing to sell out co-workers for a chance to move up the chain of command. I've seen this first-hand many times.

Years ago, I worked for an Internet company in business development. Business development is a fancy word for sales. I had a great boss who led by example and always backed up his team members. While he made it clear what the team expectations were, he also made it clear that he'd go into the trenches with us, to help us excel, and his door was always open for help. My boss was a great guy, but the people above him at the corporate office were total scumbags. They had no clue what was going on in the field, nor did they care to be informed. More concerned with keeping their easy, well-paying jobs than the pride that comes with building a company, they were completely closed to any innovative ideas. Their philosophy: Nothing was a problem if they chose not to see it that way. A philosophy I heard many times.

When sales went well, the higher-ups at corporate took full credit. They claimed their leadership and marketing tools were responsible for our collective success. When sales didn't go well, instead of taking responsibility and being proactive, they played the blame game. They feared losing their jobs, thus if they shared in the blame, their jobs were also on the line.

As usual, I was on the target list for getting fired since I'd aggravated some higher-ups by going over their heads about something. Long story short: I'd developed a more effective sales method than what people were doing before I arrived and had even proven its value in the marketplace. The problem was I did all this without the corporate office's permission. In fact, the sales strategy I'd devised had been shot down by my boss's manager, but I'd enacted the plan regardless. After generating impressive results, I informed the company's owner about the specifics. (Email is a great thing!) Every executive between the CEO and me was furious, but I was making money for the company, so they were helpless, which made them more furious.

Several months later, the company executives revised the sales commission plan, making it very difficult for the sales teams in the field to reach the monthly goals. As ridiculous as it sounds, this happens all the time, whenever a company decides they're paying the sales team too much in commissions. When sales were down for two months straight, my boss was given an ultimatum: Fire Mike or we fire you. Now most people in his situation would have sold me out, but he was an exception and refused. He was fired and one of my colleagues was promoted, then ordered to fire me. He (like most people would have) fired me...and that was the end of that lame job. The lesson learned? Integrity is only a convenience. When most people are backed up to a wall, instead of attacking their aggressor head-on, the first thing they'll do is look for someone to whom to pass the buck.

The next company I worked for provided yet another lesson in fear-based leadership. My new manager was disloyal to his people and encouraged us to sell each other out. Basically, if you complained about anything, and I mean anything, you were on an execution list and your days were numbered. One day, one of my colleagues was struggling to close some deals and brought up his frustration in a team meeting. He wasn't at all negative, just truthful about his frustration and seeking constructive feedback from the team. Our manager didn't see it that way. He'd been getting heat from the Board of Executives and needed a scapegoat. Of course, a team member voicing some frustration doesn't justify a firing, so he needed a stronger case. He called me up and tried to get me to sell out my team worker, who happened to be my friend and still is today. I contributed nothing to the manager's effort to fire my friend, but that didn't stop him - he eventually built enough of a case to fire him a week later. Because his supervisors controlled him with fear, he tried to use the same tactics with us. Still later, when he'd gotten another scare from his superiors, he fired me to save his own skin. He went on to embezzle from the company. See what happens when you lead through fear? You lose your good people and are left with slime. Then again, you are slime when using fear in the name of business leadership.

Using fear to run a company or organization is shortsighted, and ultimately ineffective. Why? Eventually, a few people will recognize fear as the illusion it is, thus rendering it intolerable as a controlling mechanism. Ultimately, as fewer people tolerate it, the power of fear dissipates. It's not a question of if, but a question of when. Further, organizations using fear as a controlling mechanism inevitably lose their smart, hard-working, independent thinkers. These people eventually conclude they don't care to put up with fear-based, petty nonsense and move on. Then, all that's left is a spineless, sycophantic following biting each other every step up the chain of command. When that's all that remains of an organization, the implosion occurs.

One of my favorite movies of all time is Braveheart. My favorite scene is the bad-ass speech William Wallace (Mel Gibson) gives before the Scots first battle with the English. The Scots are outnum-bered and justifiably scared, after all, it's not a day-job in some lame company on the line, but their very lives. Wallace understands their fear and tells the men that if they run and hide they may go on to live long lives, but their souls will die that very day on the battle-field, while they'll continue on to live lives of immense regret for not standing up for their freedom and rights. Wallace communicates to the Scots at the immortal, soul level and they come to understand that dying while standing up for what you believe in isn't anything to fear. Selling, or otherwise oppressing your soul, and living with the ensuing regret is to be feared, and shows that sometimes fear is good!

When all is said and done, I think the real fear you have is about taking responsibility for your life. There's comfort in letting other people take charge; however, it's an illusion, and a self-destructive one at that. Only you can take charge of your life and only you can stand strong in the face of fear without selling your soul to the highest, or most convenient, bidder.

Living life aggressively is about understanding it's OK to feel fear, but not OK to avoid fully living your life because of it.

ARE YOU CAPABLE OF EVIL?
YES YOU ARE

Are we born good and then corrupted by an evil society or born evil and redeemed by a good society? Maybe each of us has the capacity to be a saint or a sinner, altruistic or selfish, gentle or cruel, dominant or submissive, perpetrator or victim, prisoner or guard. Maybe it is our social circumstances that determine which of our many mental templates, our potentials, we develop.

— Philip Zimbardo, The Lucifer Effect:
Understanding How Good People Turn Evil

The Lucifer Effect: Understanding How Good People Turn Evil (Philip Zimbardo) isn't pleasant reading, but thought-provoking, and once read, you'll never see people around you in the same way again. More importantly, you'll never see yourself the same way, since the book urges you to take a hard self-inventory of who you are and what you're capable of.

While we might prefer to think we're incapable of committing acts of cruelty, the reality is we are all capable of criminal behavior and denying this merely strengthens the dark aspect lying in wait within us. As humans, we have the potential for both great compassion and great cruelty and although we must accept our more unsavory potential, this doesn't mean we must fulfill it. Living life aggressively entails taking charge of your life, and doing so requires ruthless honesty and self-awareness. I promise you this article is not a pleasant read; however, it nevertheless describes a journey each of us must eventually take. Failing to do so at your peril, and the peril of those around you.

My own journey into my heart of darkness began about ten years ago when I read a book about Bosnia's ethnic cleansing campaign. In 1995, over just a few days, Bosnian Serbian forces murdered over 8,000 people. In the book, acts of unspeakable cruelty were graphically detailed, such as fathers forced at gunpoint to rape their own daughters and women being sexually mutilated and cannibalized as they bled to death. Family members were sexually assaulted in front of one other, then everyone slaughtered. After reading dozens of these terrifying and depressing accounts I had to put the book down. How could people contain the magnitude of hatred required to commit such crimes? At the time, I couldn't stand to answer my own question, but I intuitively knew the answer would appear sooner or later.

Thankfully, I never identified with the horrors I was reading. In other words, even as I read the words on the page, never for a second did I imagine myself in such a gruesome scenario. I didn't have to question myself with would I? Could I? Since the answer was resolutely No. I am a compassionate person, to the point of experiencing depression if I haven't met my need to contribute to the well being of others.

While I feel deep compassion, Zimbardo's book forced me see the whole spectrum of my personality and I came to understand I also contain a potential for cruelty and violence - as we all do. While I've never committed Bosnian-scale violence, neither have I ever found myself in such a volatile environment, and as much as we may hate to admit it, we can't say for sure what we would do in unfamiliar circumstances. Speculate all day of what you would and wouldn't do but you'll never know for sure, and hopefully, you're never given the opportunity to find out. In order to overcome such circumstances, you must get to thoroughly know yourself and the underlying forces driving you.

We like to think of evil as something confined to a small percentage of the population. We hope that the evil ones are aberrations and somehow different from the rest of us but, in the end, most people are only as "good" as their current circumstances. Taken out of their comfort zone and placed into situations for which they're unprepared, peoples' resulting behavior can be shocking, and worse, those "people" might be you.

Let's take a look at the 1994 genocide in Rwanda. For years (and for a variety of reasons) animosity had built between the majority tribe Hutus and the minority tribe Tutsis. In 1994 this animosity reached a tipping point with the assassination of Rwandan president Juvenal Habyarimana, a Hutu. The Hutus blamed the Tutsis, in particular, Paul Kagame, a leader of a Tutsi rebel group. Kagame denied the allegations and insisted Hutu extremists were instead to blame. To this day, it's uncertain who was responsible.

After President Habyarimana's assassination, a full throttle hate campaign commenced wherein the Hutus publicly declared the Tutsis as the cause of all Hutu ills. In just over three months, Hutu death squads, bearing machetes and clubs, killed over 800,000 people - the most expeditious and horrific massacre on record. Tutsi women were typically raped prior to their murders or, if not murdered, unfortunate Tutsi women were gang-raped and physically mutilated. Set free, these victimized women made a powerful, low-tech Hutu fear campaign. This sort of sadism, and the sense of power it provides, can have a narcotic, addicting effect on the perpetrators, leading to increased frequency and intensity of assault.

How could the Hutus turn so decisively upon the Tutsis? They had co-existed for generations. From the outside, it looked as if a button were pushed and neighbors and friends suddenly became mortal enemies, but the truth is more complicated.

According to Zimbardo, the cause would be:

...hostile imagination, a psychological construction embedded deeply in [the Hutu] minds by propaganda that [transformed] the Tutsis into the enemy.

When people already blame others for their own problems, they are ripe for immoral social controls. In other words, popular media can effectively be used to direct collective aggression.

Another of the human ego's easily exploited vulnerabilities is the superiority complex. People like to think of themselves as superior to other people. In fact, on most tests in which people are compared to others, the vast majority will rate themselves as "better than average".

Superiority complexes can be dangerous weapons. Commonly wielded, sometimes concealed, sometimes not. Unfortunately, in order for people to think of themselves as better looking, better earning, better educated, stronger, or more sophisticated there must be "others" with which to compare themselves and so, put down. Considering yourself superior to others is a milder version of scapegoating, which is the lesser version of dehumanizing the "other".

Ironically, those who declare their superior status are more likely to themselves feel inferior deep down and crave acceptance within the group, to the point of desiring the group's approval by any means necessary. I've observed this phenomenon within every corporate - and otherwise - organization in which I've participated. What I've seen people willing to do in order to elevate their own status - within everyday socially acceptable circumstances, in other words, hardly civil war - is disturbing and disappointing both. The themes are uncannily similar: blaming others for your own lack, backstabbing and/or using people for your own upward mobility.

Pathological desires for superior status and group acceptance were two of the driving forces in the Rwanda genocide. In the previous era of Belgian imperialism in Rwanda, the Tutsis received preferential treatment. This went on for twenty years. During this time, Tutsis and Hutus were mandated to carry identification cards, with the Tutsis receiving more and better benefits, like access to better education and jobs. This preferential treatment generated immense resentment and jealousy among the Hutus which, over time, reached a boiling point. Later, in the aftermath of the presidential assassination, using an intensive propaganda program, Hutu leader Mayor Silvester Cacumbibito exploited the ready, latent resentment in Hutu population. This tried and true tactic of social manipulation was similarly used by Adolf Hitler in Germany and later, by the Khmer Rouge in Cambodia.

Besides identifying the Tutsis as the source of all of their ills, the Hutus further referred to the Tutsis as cockroaches. This is a well-known dehumanizing tactic which effectively increases hatred and a lack of compassion towards the perceived enemy, as a less-than-human subject is less likely to invoke feelings of sympathy or moral inhibition within the aggressor. Quoting psychologist Albert Bandura:

> Our ability to selectively engage and disengage our moral standards...helps explain how people can be barbarically cruel in one moment and compassionate the next. It is much easier to disengage your moral standards when you no longer look at your enemy as human. Once you are convinced that they are beneath you, there is no telling how much cruelty will be inflicted on the dehumanized enemy.

(Sometimes I don't know which I find more disturbing: the cruelty people commit against others or their rationalizations for the same. Moral codes seem very fluid these days.)

Another powerful factor in the Rwandan genocide was group influence. There were Hutus who did not condone their tribe's actions yet were unwilling to risk the dire consequences of taking a stand against the group. Where does individual responsibility begin and end in such ugly circumstances? Think about how many times in your life (and for far lower stakes) you've fallen under group influence. You might be sitting there on your couch, shaking your head at how dissenting Hutus did nothing to halt the atrocities going on in their name, but in the same situation - your neighbors slaying each other - are you so sure you'd behave differently? I assert you do not know what you would do.

In addition to those unwilling to go against the flow, and thus suffer potentially mortal consequences, there were other Hutus who desired the praise and accolades of the group by any means, and the more people they killed the more praise they received. The more cruelty they inflicted, the greater their status rose within the group. I'm not rationalizing their behavior, nor looking for ways to justify their actions. It's not possible to rationalize such actions; however, I mean to point out the fact that these people were not so different than any other confused people who allow their inner criminal aspects to take the lead - en masse. In a state of confusion and self-ignorance, virtually anyone is vulnerable to such an error. When such a baleful event occurs in a collective consequence, the results are amplified.

Group influence can be overwhelming, thus most people unconsciously go with the flow around them without the bother of thinking for themselves. When worldly events take a turn for the worse, the unconscious acceptance-seeking habit can be so entrenched such people easily find themselves immersed in the moment and caught up in the group accord. These are not extremists in everyday life, but "regular" people leading "regular" lives. Yet when situational forces, i.e, external circumstances, turn extreme such "normal" people, time and again through history, become barbaric without realizing the tipping point. Such is the insidious power of the collective unconscious combined with situational forces, making us only as noble as a given situation.

And so, many acts of terrible violence and cruelty are committed within the context of groups. Individuals will behave in ways they would never permit themselves on their own volition. Studies show that mental functioning literally changes in an individual "under the influence" of group pressure.

According to Zimbardo:

...when all members of a group are in a de-individuated state, their mental functioning changes: they live in an expanded-present moment that makes past and future distant and irrelevant. Feelings dominate reason, and action dominates reflection. In such a state, the usual cognitive and motivational processes that steer their behavior in socially desirable paths no longer guide people.

The above implies that living in the moment isn't necessarily a good thing, at least for someone of a lower (unconscious) state of mind. When we forget our past, we forget who we essentially are - at least the noble self - and to compound the problem, we forget what it is we've forgotten. Our higher morals, knowledge of truth, and standards, no longer apply as we succumb to immediate, primitive desires. This negative version of living in the moment (and therefore failing to consider the results of our present actions) is dangerous. Remaining amnesiac to consequences gives too much sway to any present situational forces. Whenever I'm faced with a tough decision, I mentally place myself in the future, and look back from that vantage. Is my future self proud of my choice of action - or ashamed? This method works well because anytime we stop and think about who we really are beneath our social persona, and who we want to be, and how we want to feel as that self - hopefully we make the higher, more noble, choice.

Group pressure isn't bad per se. As a member of society, you belong to a group, and just as group pressure can provoke people to terrible things, group pressure will also prevent people from doing unreasonable things. Moreover, the upside of group influence is that people often commit acts of compassion and kindness when "under the influence" of the more positive versions of social situational forces. But that is not the point of this article. To comprehend the full range of experience of the human condition we must understand how it is that so-called "normal" people are capable of terrible acts of violence. In order to do so, we might be faced with the previously unthinkable: an admission that we, too, are capable of cruelty and further denying that potential only hardens it.

Live Life Aggressively!

Zimbardo writes:

It is only by becoming aware of our vulnerability to social pressure that we can begin to build resistance to conformity when it is not in our best interest to yield to the mentality of the herd.

This process requires a ruthless self-inventory. Do you really know who you are? Have you ever taken time to analyze your past actions? While not a joyful undertaking, getting to know yourself is a forthright act of discovering what's real - something too few people pursue.

1. Think about the times when you succumbed to group pressure - have you done things of which you are not proud?
2. Is social acceptance so important to you that you reside within the collective consciousness?
3. Do you apply critical thinking in the decision process or do you rely on what others think is best for you?
4. Are you willing to speak out against the group or are you too frightened to rock the boat?

You may not feel proud of your answers, but take this opportunity anyway to pursue the process. My experience is that few people are willing to rock the boat and counter the group. Most people prefer the comfort of going through the same socially-approved-if-destructive superficial motions day to day, all the while gossiping and complaining of the unpleasant circumstances in which they find themselves.

The world is not made up of only good people, light and compassion. Life, in all its manifestation is multi-faceted, complex, and darkly shadowed. While we must discern light from dark - and good from evil - in order to do so, we must see things unfiltered by our own delusive inclinations. We must look at things in the open, and head on in order to make the higher, better, choice. Avoidance of the harsher aspects of life doesn't result in empowerment, and it's empowerment which helps us transcend the harsh and the ugly.

There is nothing wrong with attempting to see the good in any situation, but this tendency can be fraught with error - better to identify evil for what it is.

Just as alcoholics must admit they have a drinking problem before proceeding to the recovery phase, each of us must acknowledge our own inner criminal and its potential for misdeeds. By realizing your own capacity for - and possible contribution to - evil behavior, you'll remain conscious of all aspects of your personality and are less likely to unconsciously succumb to situational forces. This allows you to take inventory of the hows and whys of your past actions. Maybe you succumbed to group pressure at some point in your life and did things that you'd never do of your own volition. Maybe these were good things you did, or maybe not. All of us have succumbed to group pressure at one time or another, and most of us continue to do so, sometimes with disastrous results.

We all hope for ourselves to never experience the suffering of the people of Rwanda, Bosnia, Nazi Germany, and Cambodia, among a long list of others, but at the same time we mustn't believe we're above it all. We are just as human as everyone else in history, accountable for ourselves and the actions we take. Intimate self-knowledge transcends social influence and empowers each of us to resist social pressure and situational forces which offend our moral code.

EMBRACE COMPASSION FULLY
OR BE DESTROYED BY ANGER

Contrary to popular belief, talking about the traumas of your life may not help you to move from depression to mental health. In fact in some cases this approach may impede your natural path to resilience and recovery.
— Kelly Lambert, Ph.D author of Lifting Depression

It is often very difficult for people that have been through serious abuse at a young age to evolve in life and become truly happy. No question it is also difficult for adults. However, as an adult, you have a greater capacity to handle stress, deal with it, and move on. If you experience extreme stress as a kid you tend to suppress it. While the pain is suppressed it is still lurking deep inside affecting you on the subconscious level. You may not even be cognizant of it, but that feeling of moderate depression that always seems to follow you around could stem from such suppression.

Many people are like sleeper cell terrorists to their own health. They may walk around leading what appears to be happy, and productive lives to others, only to shock the world when they commit serious acts of self-destruction or violence. Dr. Bruce Nadler who was mentioned earlier, is such an example. This is why self-inventory and mediation are both so important. The more you know about yourself, the safer you are to yourself, and others around you. Sadly few take the time to do either.

The sooner you deal with traumas that happened to you as a child the better. Suppressing what happens never works. Eventually the floodgates break open, and it will certainly happen at a time which is not ideal. It is better to take charge and bring the issues to surface consciously and process what happened.

I don't pretend to be a mental health expert, or someone with all the answers on such matters. But I am someone that went through child abuse when I was five years old. No, it was not at the hands of my wonderful parents, or any other relative for that matter. My parents are great people who worked very hard to raise my brother, and myself, and while I am biased, I think they did a great job. Nevertheless, like anyone, they made some mistakes and one such mistake had disastrous consequences.

When I was five we lived in Korea for a few years. Often my parents had to go to work related functions and left us in the care of various nannies. Most of these nannies were very nice women and did a great job. Yet one nanny was a cruel woman that took pleasure in abusing others. She was clever and knew how to act a certain way in front of adults and also was very astute at determining what she could get away with regarding kids. Whenever my brother and I were alone she would tease us, which sounds harmless enough, but that was how it started. It was her way of testing the waters. My brother Roger was a few years older than me and was also naturally feistier than me. This worked in his favor, whenever the cruel nanny tried to do inappropriate things to him, such as forcefully kiss him on the lips, or take his clothes off, he would fight back with all his might. While he was only eight, he put up a good fight and was not worth the trouble. She wanted an easier victim that she could humiliate. She found such a victim in me. At five I was a shy quiet kid and respected adult authority completely. I was scared of adults, and did what I was told. She picked up on this and used it to her advantage.

She would take me into her quarters, strip me down, and try to dress me up like a little girl on some occasions. On other occasions she would fondle me, forcefully kiss me, and make me touch her in places that no kid should experience. Although I did not like how I felt, I also trusted adults, and thought such behavior was normal. I was never educated on what being molested is. Looking back, it was never about sex. I was after all only five years old, so clearly I could not offer anything sexually. I do not think she even viewed me as a sexual object. What she did view me as, was a person she could humiliate. The more uncomfortable I got the better she felt. The more abuse she delivered, the more powerful she felt. The more fear I had in my eyes, the more in control she felt. The fact that I belonged to a wealthy American family I am sure added to the perverse pleasure. The fact that she could look at my parents and realize they had no clue what she was doing, was also I am sure a source of power for her. In fact I know it was, as she would often look at me right in front of my parents with the same evil look she did to me in private.

When you are five years old you do not have the cognition to know what is happening. You do not have the mental skills to process such events. As a protective mechanism I think our minds block out such memories and store them deep, to be dealt with at another time. Perhaps a time in which we are more equipped to deal with such pain.

As bad as all the personal abuse was, the memory that hurt me the most was when our family dog died. My brother and I were very sad, we loved the dog. He was like another brother to us. I remember the evil nanny looking at us and laughing hysterically in our faces. She pointed her finger at us and smiled as I mourned the loss of our dog. Roger on the other hand wanted to smash her face in, and honestly I think he could have done some real damage!

I have had mild depression follow me around for most of my life. I really believe it all came from that one incident as a child. My ability to handle stress was compromised, and the weaker your stress handling abilities, the more likely you are to be depressed. The stress management hormone DHEA (Dehydroepiandrosterone), is critical for mood regulation, and according to Kelly Lambert, Ph.D more research is coming out detailing the importance of DHEA for mental health, and how it is even more critical than the highly discussed serotonin. Hormone optimization is a big passion of mine and I have researched DHEA extensively in various interviews. It keeps the stress hormone cortisol in balance and also protects the male sex hormone testosterone from being depleted by cortisol. Some studies even show, that men with higher levels of DHEA are much more courageous than men with low DHEA. DHEA is also a neurohormone and plays an important role in brain health and brain function.

While I have no lab work to support it, I think my ability to produce DHEA was compromised big time when I was five years old. Years later as an adult I always came up as low-normal for any DHEA test, even though other hormones such as testosterone where in the middle range. This was also after adopting a healthy lifestyle. It was not until I turned thirty, and had total recall of what happened to me, that I was able to finally move forward, conquer the depression once and for all, and restore my hormonal heath. This took many years of research and is the main reason why I know so much about hormone optimization. I was broken and wanted to be fixed and no one was giving me the answers or solutions that I was looking for.

One day when I was thirty, I was watching a great movie called Antwone Fisher. It is a movie based on a real life story about a troubled young man that was abused in a foster home. He was abandoned by his mother, and left at the mercy of two cruel women in a foster home. One of the women was verbally and physically abusive. The other was sexually abusive. Antwone tried to move on with his life. As an adult he joined the military in an attempt to make something of himself. Yet he always battled the anger that kept following him around. He got into fights often. While he likes women, and wanted to be in a relationship, he was understandably very uncomfortable sexually, and had intimacy issues. He wanted to be with a woman he loved but intimacy reminded him of the abuse he went through as a kid.

Antwone's mentor Dr. Jerome Davenport, played by Denzel Washington, helps Antwone deal with what happened to him.

Antwone confesses to him everything he went through. Dr. Davenport tells him that he has to go back to his hometown and find his roots. He has to find his mother and deal with all of the abandonment issues he has.

Reluctantly, Antwone does return home, and in addition to finding his mother also gets the chance to confront the women that abused him. When they see Antwone they act like everything is fine and try to hug him as if they are a loving family. Antwone holds firm and speaks his mind. He tells both that he remembers everything that happened to him. He remembers the sexual abuse, the physical abuse; the emotional abuse all of it. He stands firm and states emphatically, "It doesn't matter what you tried to do, you couldn't destroy me! I am still standing! I am still strong, and I always will be." The two abusers are speechless, as they have nothing to say. They know what they did, and they know that Antwone is right. All of their power is gone and they cower to his strength of heart.

That scene really impacted me, I found myself watching it over and over again. I would tell others about it, and they did not get it. They did not see the power I did. How could they, as they did not go through what I did? Soon after, I had total recall of what happened, and more memories keep flooding in. It was a very emotional time, and a very difficult one. Ironically it was very liberating, as it was baggage that I have been carrying my entire life.

Initially when I had total recall of the events, I wondered if they were just a fabrication of my mind. After all, I was only five years old. Perhaps it never really happened and was just a nightmare. I talked to my brother about the events. He said he remembered what I was talking about. He remembered how the nanny tried to abuse him, and how he mustered up all the strength he could manage to fight back. He remembered seeing her do inappropriate things to me but could not process what any of it meant at the time. We have a very close relationship, so he carried a lot of guilt for not protecting me. I harbor no anger towards him. He was a kid as well and did not have the power to protect me. Moreover, most of what she did to me was behind closed doors, so he had no knowledge of any of it.

As more and more memories surfaced, more and more anger came with it. I was angry at what happened, and even more angry that I could not do anything about it. After all what was I going to do, track her down in Korea? She is probably not even alive now. What good would it do anyway even if I did track her down? Living vicariously through Antwone Fisher helped ease the pain a little bit, but of course that is not enough. Movies are great for inspiring us to become greater but do not take the place of actually taking charge of our lives and living fully.

In the past I would just go into my "cave" and try to work out whatever problem I was dealing with. With the childhood abuse I felt the need to talk about it. I talked to friends, professionals, really anyone that would listen or could relate. The first disturbing thing is that the majority of people I talked to could relate personally to what I was saying. They had been through similar things themselves. One of my closest friends growing up went through almost the same thing at the hands of a baby sitter, and like me he also dealt with depression his whole life. At first talking about it did make me feel better. It was nice to unload and find people to relate to. However, after a while I found that the more I talked about it, the angrier I got. It was as if every time I talked about it, I relived it, and then had to deal with all the emotions arising each time. It got to the point where it was constantly on my mind, and made me very negative and angry all the time. I was going through some other challenges as well, which just compounded things further.

One thing that really helped me was taking care of my dog, Mona. She was my constant companion during my entire fitness career and only passed away very recently. She was a very funny dog with great energy and made me laugh often. I had to take care of her, and through taking care of her I found some solace. It made me feel good to take care of another being. Mona was abandoned by her previous owners and was at a kill shelter when a friend of mine rescued her.

She asked me to foster Mona while she looked for a full time guardian, but after a week with Mona I knew I wanted to adopt her. She made my life better instantly and was a fun dog to be around. We lived in Santa Monica, CA at the time and it was fun to walk around town with Mona. Everyone liked her. I had Mona for close to two years when I had total recall of being abused, so we had already bonded.

I could not do anything about what had happened to me, but I could do something about taking care of Mona, and ensuring that she was never abandoned or in harms way again. In fact I lived in an apartment in which dogs were not allowed (I moved there before I got Mona). One day my landlord heard Mona barking and left a nasty message on my voicemail. When I got home and heard the message I called her back instantly and went off. Mona was like my daughter, and I was not going to have any of that. When they gave me an ultimatum to get rid of Mona or move, it was the easiest choice ever. I found another apartment where dogs were welcomed.

Years later in Las Vegas, Mona developed a terrible cancerous tumor in her inner ear. The operation was very expensive and my vet was worried that I would want to have Mona put down rather than treat her, as this happened often in her office. She came and told me the situation and I could see the worry on her face when she mentioned the price. I told the vet that it does not matter what it will cost. It is the only option, I will pay it, I would never sell Mona out. The vet was nearly in tears. Long story short, Mona had the surgery, recovered and went on to live for another four happy years. She died peacefully in my arms on March 26, 2011. I did not have to put her down. She checked out on her own terms and left this world peacefully. She will never know how much she meant to me and how much she helped me through some very hard times. I am not sure I would have overcome the repressed abuse with out her.

My wonderful, then girlfriend and now wife Carol, was the most critical component in my ability to move forward. She was there for me, and was very patient as I worked through the trauma. In fact I remember one time I wanted to break up with her, as I did not feel I could handle being in a relationship at the time. Similar to Antwone I had intimacy issues and was convinced that I should just be alone. She would not have it. She would not let me push her aside. She would not let me stop her from helping me, and becoming the man I am today.

Carol was, and still is an incredible support system and I would not be the man I am today without her. Napoleon Hill in one of my favorite books ever "Think and Grow Rich" said that no man achieves greatness without a great woman by his side, and I believe that completely. Carol is a great woman and I cannot imagine my life without her. The truth is I don't want to. On the flip-side her patience paid off as she now has an incredible life as well!

You see, we don't overcome abuse by talking about it all day long. Sure it is important to talk about it initially, and unload, but at some point talking about it becomes a broken record. You have to get on with your life, but it is the way you get on with it that matters. You don't just block it out and move on. Forget about playing the distraction game or saying positive affirmations all day long. You occupy your time helping other beings. It does not have to be only other people, it can be animals as well.

When you have been through abuse you either go in the direction of compassion, self-destruction, or violence towards others. Clearly the latter two are not productive uses of your time. It is the compassion direction that is your savior. It is the only way to really empower you and move forward with resolve. Kelly Lambert Ph.D in her insightful book, "Lifting Depression", says that you win the battle against depression by occupying your time with positive and productive actions. She is not talking about daily affirmations or looking for accolades. She is talking about actions that are positive, and productive, such as healthy eating, working out, volunteering at an animal shelter, spending time helping senior citizens, helping kids that are burn victims, helping soldiers that sacrificed for all of us overseas, etc. The best way to feel great and empowered is to help people. Perhaps your way of helping others is to work hard and make a lot of money and support great organizations like Wounded Warrior and the ASCPA. That is fine. Whatever method is a fit for you, to help others is the right one. Helping others is how we ultimately help ourselves.

I am fortunate that I was able to turn my hobby of fitness into a successful career. I get to help people daily and enjoy doing it. I love what I do, and the fact that it has a positive impact on the lives of others is an incredible gift beyond measure. I wake up every day excited about my life, and I am never depressed these days. I feel strong, healthy, and confident. There is nothing that can take the place of that feeling. People that do not have it, have no clue what they are missing out on.

Life can be tough, but being self-absorbed is never the answer. It is when we immerse ourselves in the service of others that we are truly free and liberated from the wheel of suffering. While we can never get rid of anger fully, and I do not think it is healthy to do so; we can embrace compassion and make it our philosophy and guiding light through the darkness.

SECTION THREE:
HAPPINESS AND SUCCESS

THE NECESSITY OF
EXCEPTIONAL THINKING

Being "realistic" is too often an excuse for not working hard enough to improve. It also happens to be a significant source of unhappiness.

— John Eliot, PhD.

This chapter's quote comes from a great book I've been reading about the importance of exceptional thinking in achieving success and enjoying life to the fullest: Overachievement: The New Science of Working Less to Accomplish More by John Eliot. This chapter's quote reminds me of my brother, Roger, who's a perfect example of exceptional thinking.

Early in life Roger realized that being normal was not his path: his brain just wasn't made that way and there wasn't any point in denying it. In college, Roger decided to learn Japanese - this coming from a guy who failed miserably in his previous high school efforts to learn French. The difference is this: Roger was prepared to be unrealistic and busied himself learning Japanese instead of stopping to worry how very difficult it is to acquire a new language; moreover, Japanese was the language Roger was motivated to learn; everyone told him to pick an easier language but Japanese was his choice and he spent every free moment on his "word tank" acquiring new Japanese vocabulary.

Roger visited Japan many times - and for extended periods - with only the most basic Japanese language skills in his arsenal. Once you get outside Tokyo (and even in Tokyo for that matter) you'll be hard-pressed encountering people who speak even a tiny bit of English, and that's exactly where Roger spent most of his time. The first few trips to Japan were brutal: he felt like a helpless child relying on others for the most rudimentary needs, such as ordering a meal or asking for directions. Regardless, it was a great learning environment to pick up the language, as necessity can make the best teacher. Long story short: Roger gained fluency in Japanese and even lived in Japan for several years while working as a translator. Years later, when Roger's high school French tutor learned of Roger's level of Japanese fluency, she nearly fell out of her chair.

Learning Japanese is merely one example from Roger's exceptional thinking portfolio: a few years ago, Roger decided he was tired of getting ripped-off by car mechanics. He was tired of his own fear of car problems and his ignorance of how a car actually operates; thus, he decided he'd learn on his own how to fix the basic car problems. He purchased a manual for his car and went to work - in only a few short months had all the basics down. Eventually he went on to learn how to fix any and every BMW problem you could imagine. Now Roger drives with the pure confidence of knowing he can fix more-or-less any car problem that may arise and, moreover, if he does ever have to visit the mechanics, they don't stand a chance in trying to rip him off. Yet many of his so-called friends told him he'd never figure it out and thus was a waste of time to even try - a common excuse for never doing anything in life. Roger, once again, proved them wrong - which is the same path he's always blazed.

The final example I'll share of Roger's exceptional thinking happened only a few years ago: Roger was para-gliding and had a very bad accident. His leg was mangled and he was rushed to the hospital. Many of the interns told him he'd likely lose his foot or, at best, he'd walk with a gimp foot for the rest of his life. The combination of the shock from the accident with being drugged-up gave their grim assessments an ominous validity.

After a brief period of depression, Roger decided he'd make a full recovery and live a functional life in the meantime. Roger went through several operations, with the last one leaving him several months with his left leg in a cast. At the hospital, Roger told me he'd simply learn to drive with his right leg, thank you very much - which is when his nurse blurted out, "No, you won't - you can't do that!" Roger knew then, with absolute certainty, he'd learn to drive with his right leg...and went on to do so. During his entire recovery process (from initial accident to complete recovery) Roger was too focused on where he was going to let any negativity from other people affect him. When interns predicted he'd never fully recover, he'd laugh right to their face. When nurses told him what he could - or couldn't - do, he'd smile warmly, and immediately dismiss them. Such are the habits of the exceptional thinker: <u>never</u> let others tell you what you're capable of - only <u>you</u> know what you're prepared to do.

Roger's exceptional thinking has resulted in: complete fluency in Japanese; fixing any automotive or computer problem you can imagine (he even built his own computer); making a full recovery from a devastating accident that may well have permanently side-lined another, unexceptional thinker; the considerable skills to film and edit all my DVDs...and a whole list of other great accomplishments.

These days, Roger wants to break into Hollywood as a script writer. Everyone tells him it's a long-shot and he'd better have a "back-up plan" - but Roger knows back-up plans aren't for exceptional thinkers. There's only one thing an exceptional thinker wants to accomplish in life and any other option...is simply not an option. I have zero doubt he'll be a successful script writer with his solid track record of proving the naysayers wrong. Like any truly successful person, Roger's prepared to pay the price, and simply too focused on where he's going to make any pit stops in the land of doubt and failure.

Forget about being "realistic" - do you know anyone who's accomplished anything impressive by being realistic? Realistic people are boring people leading boring lives of quiet desperation. Be an exceptional thinker: if people think you're crazy you're on the right track! What's crazy is not valuing your life enough to live it to the fullest. What's crazy is letting others decide your capabilities - you declare your own potential.

USE PRESSURE
TO BE SUCCESSFUL

Many people try to avoid pressure, not realizing pressure is the thing that keeps you sharp and focused. When the pressure is on, you're not thinking about anything else but the task at hand. Let's say you're given a tough assignment due tomorrow versus a tough assignment due in a month. The former will stimulate pressure, which can create incredible levels of adrenaline and energy to get the job done, while the latter will likely result in procrastination. After all, you've got a month so there's no urgency to get started. But the problem isn't with pressure itself, only our interpretation of it. Many of us have been led to believe we perform best when we're calm and relaxed, i.e., if we feel any stress at all, it's a sign we're unprepared. The key is interpreting pressure as exhilarating rather than a debilitating stress, because pressure is a natural confidence-builder that can help us focus on the moment. When you're performing at your best, you're fully engaged in the moment, not thinking about what you'll be doing later.

Many years ago, I worked for a company and had to give a sales presentation to a group of prospects. I was told a week in advance and spent the entire week preparing for the presentation. I practiced in the mirror, memorized all my points, and did some visualization techniques in which I went over the entire lecture in my head. The point of all of this was to help me relax so that I wouldn't be stressed before the presentation. My plan was the more I practiced, the more relaxed I'd be before and during the presentation and it worked: the

171

day of the presentation I was relaxed and even somewhat excited to do it...but things took a turn for the worse when it came time to perform. Five minutes into the presentation, the pressure started cooking, which made me worry, which in turn made me go blank. I started sweating profusely as I tried to remember what to say next. The minutes felt like an eternity as I tried - to no end - moving forward with the presentation. Finally, my manager came up and saved me, which was more embarrassing than blanking out.

What did I do wrong? It wasn't lack of preparation that led to my demise that day. No, it was failure to use pressure to perform better. Instead of taking the pressure and using it, I got worried by the feeling of pressure and choked big time. Further, I took the presentation too seriously: instead of going in intending to have a good time, I just wanted to get through it. Instead of viewing the pressure as a support tool, I saw it as a sign I wasn't ready and my performance followed accordingly. I interpreted going blank as another sign I wasn't ready and shut down accordingly. The reality is public speakers go blank all the time, but they don't panic or see it as a sign of failure - something I'd learn down the road.

In The New Science Of Working Less To Accomplish More, John Elliot provides a great example of the benefits of pressure with 1950's NBA player Bill Russell. Bill was regarded as the best basketball player of the time and had the unusual habit of throwing up before every game; he was so nervous before games he puked his guts out. Oddly enough, Bill would go on to have a great game after each purging session. One day, to his surprise, he felt great before a game and didn't have the urge to vomit; the other players congratulated him. Unfortunately, he went on to have the worst game of his career. He continued playing one poor game after another and the press reported Bill was washed up and that his best days were behind him. As Bill continued having poor games, he started believing what the press was writing. The stress started building again until finally, before a game, Bill had to run into the bathroom to vomit again. He then realized the connection between pressure and performing well and felt a sign of relief. The "butterflies" Bill felt before each game were a sign he was ready to go. He went on to have an exceptional game and his team, the Celtics, won their eighth straight title.

It's ironic we avoid the very thing stacking the odds of success in our favor. Pressure is an extra source of energy kicking in whenever we do something important. It's our body's way of saying it knows that what you're about to do is important and that it's there to support you and give you what you need. I finally understood this after I bombed the sales presentation. My manager understood as well and knew the best thing for me was to get back in front of the room as soon as possible, and so I was scheduled to give a presentation the following week. The thing people fear most about public speaking is blanking out and looking foolish, but that had already happened so there was no need to fear it and, as lame as that experience was, it wasn't the end of the world. When it came time to do the next presentation, instead of trying to suppress the energy surge that came with pressure, I decided to use it and went on to give a great presentation.

I've done a lot of pubic speaking over the years and before each presentation I am always nervous. More often than not, the night before, I don't sleep well. I've taught many workshops where I didn't sleep at all the night before yet those have been some of my best. I actually enjoy the nervous energy that comes before each presentation, as I'm fully alive in those moments. The nervous energy focuses the mind and keeps you in the present, fully engaged in what you're doing. When the pressure isn't there, you can drift all over the place.

Back in 2006, I experienced the physical performance-enhancing benefits of pressure when I sponsored a kettlebell clean-and-press contest in San Diego for charity. The contest was for maximum reps with two 70-lb. kettlebells. My personal best was fourteen reps before the contest but to my surprise, at the contest I easily blasted through fourteen reps and finished off with nineteen reps. I think I could've gotten more reps if I'd focused on the task at hand, but I couldn't believe how light the bells felt and started thinking about it around rep eighteen. Sure enough, rep nineteen felt very heavy and it was the last rep. Still, the pressure of performing with people watching was a real energizer. For this same reason, I'm always stronger at my workshops than at my own workouts.

The pressure that comes along with other people watching can result in enhanced performance - if you let it. The key, again, is to welcome the energizing pressure and transfer the energy to whatever you're doing instead of allowing it to stress you out. For once the energizing pressure is created, you have to use it - failure to do so results in plain old stress. Thus if you have to give a lecture and decide to cancel last minute due to the high level of pressure that you're interpreting as stress, your end result will be even more stress. Once energy is created, it can't be destroyed, only transferred, or in this case, displaced. Failing to transfer the energizing pressure results in internalizing it, so instead of pressure turning into exhilaration, it turns into destructive stress.

What's more stressful than feeling pressure, is feeling no pressure at all. As human beings we're born to push the limits of what we are capable of and to take risks, that's where a deeper experience of life is found. There's no excitement in taking the path of least resistance and avoiding growth opportunities, yet many of us look hopefully toward future days in which we'll no longer have pressures, failing to realize that pressure is what makes us feel completely alive. Think of those times in your life wherein you were given a difficult task and rose to the occasion, remember the super-energizing feeling of accomplishment and vitality that followed? We end up talking about them in the past tense to keep the feeling of being alive going, but that's not enough. The pressure that vitalizes us comes from playing the edge of the unknown, not from what we've already accomplished.

Think of times when you surprised yourself accomplishing something that you didn't realize you were capable of. Those are life's amazing moments, yet instead of embracing them we'll retract, trying to avoid the pressure.

What is the excitement in watching a movie in which you already know what's going to happen? Your life is no different. Next time you feel pressure, welcome it and embrace it. Enjoy the feeling of being fully alive and welcome the feeling as often as possible.

BEING A GREAT
TEACHER IS NOT EASY

"The true teacher knocks down the idol that the student makes of him.
— *Rumi*

It is very tough to be a great teacher. We all have egos, and generally teachers have stronger egos than other people. Regardless, if a teacher cannot humble oneself, and be a student, then the teacher no longer has value. Some teachers like the authority and power that comes with having a following. Being a teacher myself, I know how intoxicating it can be, to be in front of a room of students, having their full attention. In addition, my students pay a good amount of hard earned cash to work with me. I do not take the responsibility lightly, and I work my ass off to put on great workshops. In fact, if I am not drained the day after a workshop then I know I held back and did not put my best effort forward. If I do not get testimonials from my workshop participants then I did not put in my best effort. Regardless, being a good teacher is not about acquiring praise, or encouraging others to follow what you say blindly. In fact the greatest gift that a teacher can provide is the lesson of learning, and critical thinking. A real teacher encourages students to seek out the truth on their own. A real teacher does not allow students to become worshippers and idolaters.

Life is always a learning process, no matter what the field of study is, and when you stop learning you stop growing. A teacher has a responsibility to encourage growth and send the students forward when he or she no longer has anything to teach. Great teachers take pleasure in their students surpassing them. Trying to hold one's students back is similar to a parent trying to impede the growth of their children. Such behavior is reprehensible!

One of my favorite books is *Dune* by Frank Herbert. Frank Herbert was a brilliant man that had an incredible imagination. His characters come alive in his book and his stories are clearly made for adults. No simple good and evil battles with a condescending, simplistic message. Herbert understood how complicated it is to be a human being and do the right thing. Being a leader is very difficult, as even the best intentions can go horribly wrong. In the first *Dune* book, the main character Paul goes from being a naive young man, to the strong and powerful leader of a repressed society. He leads a successful revolution against a corrupt emperor. *Dune* ends happily, Paul takes the place of the tyrannical emperor and justice is realized. His journey from boyhood to manhood was filled with trials and tribulations, just as every person's journey to becoming a self-actualized being is. In the third *Dune* book, Paul loses control of his empire. His followers kill in his name and he cannot do anything to stop it. He has become a figure head, and a religion is created around him. He, as an individual, only has the illusion of power and what is done in his name is too much for him to take. The final straw is the death of his wife as she gives birth to his children (twins). Unable to handle the depression he walks off into the desert to die.

Paul had the best of intentions. He was a good man, who led an oppressed people to freedom. Unfortunately, the oppressed people become the new oppressors, and he could not do anything to stop it. His followers worshipped him as a god, and at the same time no longer recognized the flawed humanity in him. They put their blinders on and there is nothing more dangerous than a desperate society of blind followers. Any history student can confirm that.

With being a teacher comes immense responsibility. You have to make it clear to you're students that you do not have all of the answers. You have flaws as well and the great thing is that it is not a big deal. We live in such an artificial world that many people yearn for depth and real communication. We are so hungry for something real that our actions as a society have become desperate. The fact that "Reality TV" is so popular says it all. Many of us are so repressed that the inevitable boiling point is only around the corner and when it finally breaks through the flood gates, all hell breaks loose. When we repress our emotions and feelings we always end up depressed. Eventually depression, which is internal anger, often leads to outward anger and the consequences can be disastrous.

In order to be more effective teachers we have to show honest vulnerability, and honest flaws. The illusion of perfection is just that: an illusion. Celebrities are not better then you and no, they do not have all the answers. People with immense wealth are not better than you and nope they do not have the answers either. With the solving of any problem comes new problems. When you make a lot of money you solve the problem of not having money. Now you have to worry about losing you're wealth and people being friends with you only for your money. When you lose fat and build muscle, you solve the problem of being overweight and unhealthy. Have no doubt that other problems are just around the corner.

Life is a constant battle of solving problems and facing new ones. Each time we solve a problem we grow immensely. When we think we no longer have any problems we are only kidding ourselves. Ignoring a problem or pretending that it does not exist will not make it go away. While this is unacceptable for anyone that is interested in personal growth and living a full life, it is completely reprehensible for a teacher to pretend that problems do not exist. If you run a company and your top six people leave, it is highly unlikely that the six people who left were the problem. It is however highly likely that the organization that they left is the problem. Try to avoid that reality all you want. Just do not believe for a second that it is not likely the truth.

The final thing that a teacher must do is admit mistakes. Just as a good teacher is aware that students make mistakes. A good teacher must be aware that he or she not only makes mistakes but will always make mistakes. Does this mean that a teacher that makes mistakes is not a good teacher? Of course not. In baseball if you hit the ball three times out of every ten tries you're a superstar! This means that players who miss the ball the majority of the time are the best around. Their flaws are open to all of their fans yet the fans still love them. If professional baseball players can be superstars with their obvious flaws, a teacher in any field can be a superstar as well with the admittance of mistakes. Bottom line is: your students see your mistakes anyway, so take responsibility and ownership of your actions.

Sending the message to your students that you are infallible and perfect is a disservice to say the least. Sending the message that you're too good to get your hands dirty only sends the message that you're not a good teacher. As we have all heard many times a great teacher leads by example. The saying "Do as I say, not as I do" is perfect for teachers that do not deserve to be teachers.

Whenever a teacher is too good to be true, go with your instincts. We all know when someone is genuine, and when someone is disingenuous. Whether we choose to go with our instincts is another story. Perception may be reality. However, at the end of the day, reality is reality, and the truth can only be held back for so long.

Be a great teacher and a great person by laying it on the table. Do not be afraid to be vulnerable and imperfect. Hell, do not be afraid to be afraid. Life is scary and avoiding that truth does not make it any less scary. Leave distraction methods to magicians. Work some real magic in your life by being an authentic person and surrounding yourself with authentic people. Life is too short to live a lie. Live the truth!

JEALOUSY IS A WASTED EMOTION

If you are discontented but unwilling to give up what is holding you back, you will have to admit that it is you who has chosen to reject success and to abandon the dream of being all of the best you can be. If this is so, you can stop getting jealous whenever you see other people around you succeeding in the life you thought you wanted for yourself.

– Chin-Ning Chu,
from her book Do Less, Achieve More

Over the years, I've realized you can't want success for others more than they want it for themselves. You can give someone the tools they need for success but if they don't use those tools and follow through, success will always evade them. You can send them opportunity after opportunity and introduce them to all the right people, yet success will always evade them. Why are some people not prepared to lay the groundwork for success? Who knows? As motivational speaker Jim Rohn says, "It's one of the mysteries of the universe."

The main reasons people fail to succeed? Lack of self-responsibility and self-awareness. You have to take charge of your life and take responsibility for your success. It's not anyone else's job but your own to be successful - as long as you rely on other people and relinquish responsibility, you won't experience success. No matter what others do for you, if you don't take responsibility for yourself, it's all in vain.

I once had an online client who signed up for a three-month program. I put a program together for him and never heard back...until six months later when he emailed me complaining I'd let him fall off-course and that it was my fault he didn't succeed. In his world, it was my fault. After all, he'd done his part in paying for the program, right? Wrong: you can't buy success; success is earned through action. Yes, you can buy knowledge, which is critical to success - but certainly not everything, there are plenty of knowledgeable people out there in all manner of fields who aren't successful, due to lack of right action.

Lets get back to the client: the client didn't follow the program designed for him and never sent me his training journal. I require all my clients to keep a training journal and to send me that journal every Friday for review. This keeps the client and I both engaged and committed; however, I clarify up front that if you neglect to email your journal I won't be emailing you.

I'm not the type of trainer who'll come to your house and wake you up in the morning or call everyday to motivate you, that's not what "Aggressive Strength" is all about. I want to work with people who are ready to make a change and are self-motivated. These people require guidance, direction, and a personalized program to fit their lifestyle. That's the service I provide - not coddling people and treating them like children.

The online client who didn't follow through on his end chose to blame me for his lack of success, even though he chose to neither follow the program designed for him nor to send his journal for feedback. While he was motivated enough to pay for a training program, he wasn't motivated enough to take the real-world action and responsibility necessary for his success. Many people feel that if they're paying someone for a service, that person is now responsible for their success. Well, it doesn't work that way: no one else can do this work for you. You can't drop the "success burden" upon others and expect positive results, such a mentality is for losers! The best others can do for you is act as guides and consultants, supporting your getting on track and staying there. At the end of the day, you have to put in the work.

Next, lets talk about self-awareness: what do you know about yourself, and what are you capable of? What is it about yourself that holds you back? Plenty, probably, if you take an honest appraisal. Yes, you have to take a ruthless look at yourself and address your weak points. Of course, this means actually accepting that you have weak points and then, more importantly, doing something about them. The former is often harder than the latter as it's easy to wear blinders and blame circumstances or the world for your own lack of success - people do it every day.

One common trait holding back unsuccessful people is their jealousy of others' successes. The unsuccessful can't stand to see people do what they themselves didn't have the stones for. Whenever someone acquires success, the jealous people get angry. What they fail to realize is this: successful people are prepared to pay the price of success, thus any jealousy of that success is both petty and counterproductive. Jealousy is a wasted emotion which misplaces your focus. Again, the focus needs to be not on others, but inward - on what you are prepared to do. Your own lack of success isn't anyone else's fault, and your wasted jealous energy won't change this.

Rather than feeling jealousy around successful people, a better use of vital energy is feeling inspiration - realizing that what others can do, so can you. It boils down to that word no one wants to hear: sacrifice. What are you prepared to sacrifice for success? You can't watch four hours of TV everyday, then waste four more hours surfing the Internet, then complain that you don't have time for creating success. When you take time to assess your situation and your daily habits, what becomes clear is what you're not doing and thus, what needs to be done. The only question left is - what are you prepared to do now?

One thing is certain: days turn into weeks, weeks into months, and months into years. Before you know it, you've repeated the same year over and over again as a decade's passed you by. But you always have this choice: if you're content where you are, stay there and continue with your daily routine - or, choose a new direction for yourself and finish what you once started.

BEING RISK ADVERSE
MAKES YOU SUCCESS ADVERSE

Human beings are incredibly adept at rationalizing any line of behavior. We decide what we want (whether rationally or emotionally) then go into lawyer mode amassing the support material necessary to justify our actions. We are incredible defense attorneys when it comes to what we want. The problem is we're often not honest about what we want and further, what we think we want isn't the real thing.

People email me all the time asking for business advice. They want to get into the fitness business but always have an array of excuses why the present isn't a good time. They desire motivation to jump into the business and hope I have the magic words to thrust them into action.

They're deluding themselves about what they really want: They don't really want to get into the business, it's just the passing thought excites them. If they were ready to make a change and jump in, they'd do it without rationalizing why. People ready to make a change, make the change, then rationalize why they made the change, not the other way around.

People make dramatic changes in their lives when they're fed up internally or feel forced by external circumstances. They prefer to stay in their comfort zone, reinforcing all their reasons for avoiding change. Big changes typically occur dramatically, not gradually: one day you're working in some office, bored out of your mind, and the next week you're engaged in the business you've always dreamed of

184

doing but were simply not committed to pursuing. One day, you're fifty pounds overweight, and the next year you're lean and in shape. A year isn't a long time - big changes can happen within a year given determination and tenacity.

Major life changes are often thrust upon us. For example, fitness has been my passion for many years: I got hooked in 1992, and spent most of my time test driving fitness programs and reading every training book and magazine I could find. (I continue these practices, reading twenty or so training books a year, and too many articles to count.) Fitness was my passion, yet didn't become my occupation until 2002. From 1996 to 2002 I worked at various jobs I couldn't care less about. Why? Because I was influenced by others, neither prepared to take charge of my life nor make my own decisions about what I wanted to do.

Every time I considered quitting my job and plunging into the fitness business I found many reasons to justify staying put. I refer to this period of my life as a time in which I wasn't doing what I wanted to do, but in reality I was doing what I wanted. Truly, if it hadn't been what I wanted, I'd have taken the steps to change. While the job was boring, it was easy, providing me a comfort zone and a steady, every-two-week, paycheck. Why would I give that up to take on the risky proposition of self-employment? I didn't give it up and it wasn't until I got fired, felt completely fed up, that I decided I was finally ready to push forward and not look back.

I feel irritation around risk-averse people who lack the courage and tenacity to do what they really want with their lives, yet I know the reason I feel irritation is because I used to be those people and they remind me of a part of myself I don't like. I know what it's like to stay in the comfort zone, performing meaningless work day after day. I've been there, I know what it's like to know what you really want and still find excuse after excuse to stay put. I've been there and my discomfort reminds me it's easy to return there.

We each have an inner coward (for lack of a better word) discouraging us from risk taking and life's other active engagements.

This coward has a subtle, albeit extremely persuasive voice, but if you give in you've done so of your own volition. No one makes you live a life of passivity (certainly not in America where possibilities are endless) and if you don't fight the voice of the "passive way", you'll find your life becoming ordinary, i.e., never leaving the comfort zone. No, living it up two weeks of each year on your scheduled vacation isn't enough (try as you might to make those brief vacations distracting) and "living for the weekends" is nothing less than pathetic.

In their formative years, businesses typically display innovation, courage and persistence. Over time, they tend to stall as the people running them become more comfortable and risk-averse. Gather seven people, all sharing the same belief system, in a meeting room together and you're guaranteed a non-innovative time! All they do is reinforce their mutual beliefs and nothing original comes of it. This happens with companies and organizations all the time.

When I entered the fitness field in 2002, I decided to focus on kettlebell training. I attended a Pavel Tsatsouline kettlebell course sponsored by a company called Dragon Door. A few months after taking the course I started by kettlebell focused business and hit the floor running. I focused my business model around kettlebell workshops and was the first person to do so. No one else at the time was making their full-time income as a kettlebell instructor nor was anyone presenting kettlebell workshops. Kettlebells were a ground-floor opportunity but there weren't many people to invite to the party! Probably there weren't more than one hundred people who owned kettlebells in 2002. Most of my early seminars brought less than four hundred dollars (which is less than the cost of a single registration these days.) My first workshop in 2002, in Los Angeles, a whopping three people attended.

I didn't make much money back them, but it was an exciting time, the first time in my life I was making money doing something I was excited about. Over the next few years the business grew and in 2005 I took a huge step forward, enjoying ample income ever since.

It's a blessing doing that which you love and making a great income at it.

Over the years, I've become more efficient, gradually shifting from a workshop-emphasis business model to a product-focused business model, resulting in a welcome passive income - this means I make money while not actively "working".

I love the passive income business model but if you're not careful, it recreates the comfort zone. I'm not materialistic by nature, so I'm unmotivated to work hard in order to buy fancy cars and big houses. The house we live in is fine and the same Honda Civic I've been driving for years still gets the job done. Thus, materialistic goals are useless to urge me out of my comfort zone. In early 2006 I fell into a comfort zone and knew I had to change things around.

In 2006 I decided to break with Pavel's organization and go off on my own. Once I was on my own, I learned more about marketing my own company and taking further charge of my destiny. It was another exciting time, resulting in more professional and personal growth. In spite of all this, in getting the business on track I fell into another comfort zone.

I decided to break out of the comfort zone by taking on a bigger project : The Boys are Back in Town workshop, where I teamed up with long-time friends and colleagues, Steve Cotter, Steve Maxwell and Nate Morrison, in presenting a two-day workshop in Las Vegas. The four of us had worked together with Pavel but never collaborated on a workshop of our own in which we did everything from promotion, to registrations, to instruction. This was our opportunity to present a workshop of our own ideas without any restrictions. It was also a chance to create an unprecedented offering.

Someone I go to for business advice is my friend, Tim Larkin. In addition to his self-defense expertise, Tim is a marketing master and he recommended I videotape The Boys are Back In Town workshop and produce a DVD set for sale. It was a great idea and it paid off handsomely. More importantly, it provided an opportunity to create an exciting offering: Not only would our workshop attendees benefit from this great seminar but they'd also receive the ultimate souvenir of a DVD of the workshop itself. No more information overload wherein you go home retaining only 10% of the information presented. Now, the possibility of 100% retention became reality, since you can watch the DVD set as many times as you wish.

I paid for the production of the DVD myself and also gave every attendee a free copy of the finished product. This offer was not included within the promotion copy when people signed up, so they had no idea beforehand. When I announced at the workshop that we were taping the event and everyone in attendance would get a complementary copy, people clapped in excitement.

While the workshop was a huge success, the accompanying DVD set proved to be a bigger success and remains the gift that keeps on giving. The combination of workshop plus DVD is an incredible offering; something I think will become a standard in the fitness industry.

Breaking from Pavel's organization and producing the The Boys are Back in Town project were both risks that paid off well for everyone involved and pulling it off was a huge rush.

Life is an obstacle course of comfort zones and just because you've broken out from one comfort zone doesn't make you free and clear. Comfort zones creep up on you when you're distracted and before you know it, there you are, comfortable, again. In order to escape the comfort zone, you must take on discomfort - and that means risk! And risk means things won't always go your way. Destiny favors the bold, but you may have to exhibit boldness for a good long while before the payoff. Detach yourself from the anticipated fruits of your labors for just a moment and realize that risk taking in itself is exciting. Risk taking in itself is the juicy fruit, not the paper you're vying for.

Wherever you are in life right now, it's exactly where you want to be. (Yes, there may be an exception or two - so don't flood my email box with complaints describing your unique situation.) The bottom line? If you're not doing what it takes to improve your current unhappy situation it's because you don't want to. There's always something you can do to make things brighter, the key is you actually have to want it.

WILL YOU LET A "KNIFE" PREVENT YOU FROM CONQUERING YOUR GOAL?

You must be relentless. If this were a fight to the death, would you let a dagger in a rib stop you?

— Octavio Consone, Highlander: The Series

You'll never be a professional in life's game until you'll willingly take a (metaphorical for some, literal for others) knife to the gut...then keep pushing forward. Your focus on what you want must be such that you don't even feel that knife, and even if you do, your determination never waivers. If it does, you're still an amateur, not yet ready to progress further. If you think you have all the time in the world to pursue your goals, think again. The reality is the clock is ticking fast, and if you don't take action now, you probably never will. There will always be excuses, but successful people make opportunities, not excuses, and that's more reality for you.

You have to become self-actualized to achieve any meaningful success, no matter your goal. If you don't know yourself, and thus your potential, genuine success will ever evade you - and rightly so.

Newsflash: Suffering, no matter how moderate or severe, is a part of achieving any meaningful goal. There's no way to avoid it and never has been. No amount of pep rally - Tony Robbins seminars can prevent suffering. Fuzzy, positive-thinking slogans won't inure you. Emailing me for free advice on how to skirt suffering on the way to success will not only not spare you, but invite more suffering! Suffering is a critical component of life and success. On a basic physiological level, we require the stress hormone, cortisol, to thrive, if we don't produce enough we can actually die. Stress makes us stronger and without it, our adrenal glands function at a low level. Our goal is not avoiding stress, but managing it, and even using it to our advantage.

Make no mistake: you will suffer on the way to achieving any meaningful goal. Like every other successful person, you must pay your dues. While the current economic bailout indicates seemingly free rides, those relying on being bailed out have lost the game; they will never be self-actualized.

As Shakespeare said, "Cowards die many times before their deaths, the valiant never taste of death but once." Living your life in fear is slavery to fear and thus cowardly. Yet there is nothing wrong with feeling fear. Fear is often unconscious exhilaration, and it's those moments when you are most fully alive. Fear brings a sharpness that can be used to your advantage - if you follow through with worthy action. Use fear as an excuse to avoid expansion and reap what you sow.

Let's look at some exemplary people who not only didn't resist the pain but pushed through:

Mixed martial arts legend Randy Couture once received a broken arm while blocking a kick from opponent Gabriel Gonzaga, resulting in a separated ulna, a heinous injury which didn't prevent him from defeating Gonzaga by TKO and retaining his title.

NBA legend Michael Jordan pushed through the finals with a case of severe flu and came through for his team. I'm not a basketball fan, but I remember watching that game in awe as Jordan sucked it up and did what it took to play at an elite level despite his illness. He worked harder in that run-down state than someone pumped up and primed. Lesson: People who wait for the "perfect" time to act never take action. Losers make excuses while successful people make opportunities.

When you feel like crap, you must not only take action but do a great job! This is the true measure of your determination. Anyone can work hard under optimal conditions, although few even do this much. Try this: push through even when everything is crashing down around you and see what you're made of. This is survival-of-the-fittest time: thrive or die off. It's easy to feel the enthusiasm when the going is fun, but professionals continue pushing through once the fun is long departed and nobody else cares anymore. Get past the amateur, glazed-eye stage and re-evaluate how much you still desire your goal.

This article's knife analogy comes from a terrific episode of Highlander: The Series. For those of you unfamiliar with either the movie, Highlander, or the ensuing television series, it's about immortals who must fight each other to the death...only one man emerges victorious. Difficulty: the only way to win is to chop off the head of your opponent. OK, it sounds like a cheesy concept thought up by Dungeons & Dragons uber-nerds, but the original Highlander is a movie classic (albeit not so much the crappy sequels) and seasons two through five of Highlander: The Series were superb, full of real drama and complex characters.

In the episode "Duende" occurs a flashback wherein the main character, Duncan McLeod, learns a valuable lesson from his mentor, Octavio Consone. While engaged in sword fighting practice, Octavio stabs Duncan in the rib to make his point. Duncan, shocked, protests that the stabbing was unnecessary but Octavio retorts that in order to win, one must be relentless, even willing to take a knife to the ribs for victory. He goes on to say Duncan has good instincts and won't make the same mistake twice. This is a foreshadowing of what comes later in the story...

Many years later, Duncan and Octavio are now enemies and fighting to the death. Octavio is winning the fight until Duncan cunningly disarms him by pulling Octavio's sword into his own stomach. Octavio, unable to defend himself, loses his head. Duncan fully exploited the opportunity even though it engendered considerable personal suffering. Despite his immortal status, he still feels physical pain, like everyone else, and further, welcomed that pain as part and parcel of his victory.

Experiencing a life or death situation teaches you more about yourself than anything else. Unfortunately, what you learn may be disappointing, but personal growth begins with honest self-assessment. I think everyone needs at least one dance with death to truly value life. I, myself, only completely committed to my goals after nearly succumbing to a virulent case of pneumonia in 2002. That experience at the edge taught me a lot about myself and I've never looked back. It was a knife to the gut (though not the only one) and I received it, pushed through, and consequently grew stronger.

While few of us will be forced to literally push through a stabbing, such symbolically intense events aren't outside the realm of possibility for any of us and certainly, we will all face tough times on our way to self-actualization and no matter what you achieve or acquire in the world, without self-actualization, it's meaningless.

Have you taken a metaphorical knife to the gut?

IS EXPERIENCE OVERRATED?

Extensive research in a wide variety of fields shows that many people not only fail to become outstandingly good at what they do, no matter how many years they spend doing it, they frequently don't even get any better than they were when they started.

— Geoff Colvin, Talent Is Overrated

The above passage, from Colvin's book, really gave me some food for thought. It may be counter-intuitive to think of those with more experience as inferior to those with less experience, given the same job, but when you think about it, it really isn't so surprising. Most people exist on autopilot, learning only enough to get the job in the first place, and then just enough more to keep that job. Once they've achieved the lowest rung of competence, that same level of excellence - rather, mediocrity - is repeated for years on end. On the other hand, those few people driven to excel in a profession will always seek ways to improve themselves and their performance. These people work hard year after year and a few years of this applied, conscious effort - what Colvin calls deliberate practice - is more meaningful than a decade of going through the motions.

Let's look at this concept closer. You might think it impossible to not get better at something after accumulating years of experience, yet proof of the opposite is abundant. For example, take a moment to observe some of the regular members of your local gym. Notice where they are now, then, at year's end check again. It's highly likely any positive change will be negligible, and this can (and usually does) go on for years. Worse, there's a good chance you are one of these people, so it's time to wake up and focus. Logging years of drone work isn't going to cut it.

The above is why I detest statements like...just showing up is 80% of success or the equally false...fake it till you make it. Here's the truth: Showing up isn't enough for success. As you've just observed yourself, people "show up" at the gym everyday year after year with nothing to show for it. You must replace going through the motions aka "showing up" with a genuine desire to improve. To do this requires a rigorous self-assessment of whether what you've been doing is working and whether you actually want to invest yourself in improving. The road to an improved version of yourself requires self-knowledge and discipline, not faking it. That which is real will always come out on top over that which is fake. Yes, I'm referring to the current economy, wherein instead of taking charge of problems, people have tried to pass the buck and blame others which is pathetic but beyond the scope of this article!

All right, let's get back on topic. From infancy into early adulthood we learn to progress and adapt. Then, somewhere along the way to adulthood, we slip into maintenance mode, and for some people, maintenance mode is a life story. Imagine being in the first grade for ten years: does ten years of experience in first grade bring superiority over someone in tenth grade? Of course not! The person who progressed from first to tenth grade had to apply a deliberate practice to get there. Remaining in first grade for ten years merely requires "showing up" to repeat what's already been experienced. While a decade spent in first grade may seem ludicrous, people often apply equally ridiculous logic to their own lives. Just because you're getting older doesn't mean you're getting better at anything, and stagnation - at any age - is deleterious to growth and realizing your ultimate potential. Someone putting in three years of deliberate practice will surpass anyone with accumulated time in the comfort zone.

It's not that experience is without value. Experience is critical to excellence in any field or endeavor, but we must separate experience in deliberate practice from experience within the comfort zone. The former is a result of focused effort to improve the desired skill(s) while the latter prefers to only go through the motions. But you never get better at anything by just going through the motions; getting better at something requires a focus on what you're doing as well as an effort to do it better. Few people do this. Most people will settle for mediocrity, but highly successful people seek more and are consequently willing to do the necessary work.

One thing I've found incredibly valuable for my own growth is feedback from other people. I'm fortunate to have many friends in the business who provide honest feedback, as well as intelligent customers who take the time to provide feedback. Feedback is crucial for growth, since it provides multiple perspectives.

When I started my training business in 2002, I took massive action to get started up, including presenting as many kettlebell workshops as possible and writing tons of sports articles. No doubt, this experience resulted in me getting better at both workshops and articles, but my improvements weren't dramatic until the feedback started coming in. Specifically, I got better at workshops merely by presenting a few, and the more I did, the more my confidence grew; however, I became too confident around the tenth workshop.

This workshop took place in Northern Virginia and was billed as a beginner's workshop; however, I was so excited about the new techniques I'd been learning and applying to my own personal workouts that I decided to bombard the students with everything I had.

Rather than picking a few exercises and teaching them thoroughly, I bombarded the attendees with one exercise after another...and yet another. The few more experienced, students in attendance loved it, but the majority of the group was driven into survival mode and a few left halfway through, since they couldn't keep up. My good friend, top Northern VA Kettlebell trainer Dylan Thomas, who was assisting me, refers to this day as...when Fonzie jumped the shark.

Fortunately for me, Dylan is a straight shooter and provided the ruthless feedback I needed: the workshop was too much show-and-tell and lacked focused instruction. This helped me to pull in the reins and get back on course. I returned to the basics and focused on teaching the students an array of basic movements rather than showing them all I'm capable of doing. Lesson learned: people don't sign up for workshops to watch your personal workout (no matter how impressive) - they sign up to learn and improve their own training.

Once you shift the focus from yourself to the student, and continue to focus on what you can do to improve their experience - you're on the right track. These days, after each workshop I look at what can be improved and how to better, more efficiently, teach skills for maximum retention. This same focus on improvement is how I came up with the workshop-DVD concept, wherein attendees receive a DVD to take home from the each workshop. Sometimes the DVD is the actual course they've just taken (as with The Boys are Back in Town and Collision Course) and other times it's a DVD of equal content to that just covered (e.g., Beginner Kettlebell Workshop). This original (and incredible) offering allows you, the student, to achieve 100% retention, since you can review the DVD whenever you like in your deliberate practice to master everything demonstrated at the workshop. The feedback is in and people love this combination.

Another feedback tool I've found invaluable is video footage of myself instructing. If I'd taped every workshop from day one, my rate of improvement would have tremendously accelerated. While that's no reason for regret, what I learned from my first taped workshop, The Boys are Back in Town, was a watershed. My brother, Roger, videos and edits all my DVDs, staying at my house while he completes the editing process. This allows me to review the raw footage before it goes to the final copy and it's funny how my recollection of my instruction is so different from what actually occurred - sometimes dramatically different! For example, the panel discussion segment of Boys never made it to DVD because, in my mind, I succinctly answered each question while the reality is it took me forever to get to the point. Understandably disappointed with myself, I applied this feedback to improving Collision Course and I'll continue putting in the deliberate practice to further improve future productions.

- Have you applied deliberate practice to your career, working hard to increase your efficiency and value?

- Do you put in the required research each year to increase your knowledge base? Or do you exist upon that which you already know?

These are tough questions, but if your desire is to break from the herd and advance (in any field) you're going to have to be honest with yourself. Success requires more than experience - people can settle into their experiences, but life is more meaningful when you're not settled in.

I NEVER SAVED
ANYTHING FOR THE SWIM BACK

You want to know how I did it? This is how I did it, Anton: I never saved anything for the swim back.

-- Vincent, from the film Gattaca (1997)

One of my all time favorite movies is the classic, Gattaca, a thought-provoking story if you take the time to digest the multiple messages within. Unfortunately, most people watch it and return to their quiet and miserable life. I'm forever amazed by the lack of inspiration people display with all the powerful examples and sources of inspiration out there and available to all. But, save that rant for a later date...

Gattaca depicts a world of the future ruled by genetically superior humans. It's no longer about race or wealth, but about who has the best genes. If you're not born with the right genes for a desired occupation, then you've zero chance of acquiring that occupation. Neither how hard you work, nor any other effort you might put in matters - you're shut out entirely and must accept your lot. Ironically, in our society, people suffer from self-limitations more than any limitation the collective puts upon them.

Vincent Freeman (a masterful Ethan Hawke) decides he's unwilling to accept these oppressive societal limitations and figures out a way to achieve his dreams. Vincent's lifelong dream is space travel and he refuses to concede defeat. He assumes the identity of Jerome Morrow (Jude Law), who has the necessary genetic profile and is willing to sell it. Jerome is in a wheel chair, has lost his zeal for life and thus no longer cares about benefiting from his superior genetics.

While Gattaca has many powerful scenes, fans know the most powerful of all is the swim scene: Vincent has a brother, Anton, genetically superior both mentally and physically; however, being born with his gifts, Anton never develops either Vincent's mental toughness or tactical thinking skills. Growing up, Vincent and Anton competed with each other in ocean swimming to see who could swim the farthest out from the shore. With his superior physical genetics, Anton always won; however, as Vincent matures he develops human spirit, a quality which no one is born with but is instead realized through suffering and perseverance - something about which the genetically gifted Anton knows nothing.

As adults, they once again engage in the swimming contest and this time, to Anton's surprise Vincent wins. Anton, flabbergasted, asks Vincent how he did it. Vincent replies: I won because I never saved anything for the swim back. Though genetically superior, Anton is a slave to his genetics; Vincent wins by transcending genetics. Anton's genetic assets thus become liabilities, causing him to lose the swim contest. Vincent, who's spent his lifetime working within enforced limitations, never lets institutionalized societal rules hold him back. Born with weakness, Vincent spends his life over-coming weakness and never gives up. Space travel becomes his obsession - as your goals must obsess you in order to excel.

Swimming out without concern for how you will get back to shore is a metaphor for pursuing your dreams without any back-up plans. Too many people opt out before truly getting started by telling themselves they can do something else when and if their dream career fails to thrive. Is this your mentality? If so, don't bother with your dream career because you've already missed. As the sage warfare strategist Sun Tzu wrote: the winner and loser of a fight is already determined before the fight starts. If you've already got your fall back job lined up in case your dream career fizzles, your fight is already determined...and you've lost! Instead, you must be so single-mindedly focused on what you want that even the idea of doing anything else is never conceived. When something isn't an option, it will never obstruct you. Excuses are unacceptable: This is do or die time and those unprepared to handle such hardcore mentality must fall back and prepare instead to accept a self-created, mediocre experience of life.

There are infinite excuses and rationalizations why now is the imperfect time. There are countless people to call you unrealistic. There are eternities in which, with no one to motivate you in pushing forward, you must be self-reliant. And so what? What else is new? No matter if they're big or small, excuses are excuses. You can thank me for the truth: You - and only you - are in charge of your life. Failure is always entirely your own fault. With an honest self-assessment comes freedom and you have the freedom to change your life...if you're willing to pay the price. Are you willing pay the price?

I can already hear people arguing that wanting a thing badly - and even working hard to achieve it - doesn't mean you will get it. While that may be true, they're missing the point. Genuine victory comes not from achieving a given goal but in refining yourself in the process. This is something that can never be taken away from you. Vincent's victory wasn't in beating Anton in a swim contest, no, it was the person he became in the process of doing so.

Are you willing to swim out so far without worrying how you'll get back?

WAITING FOR PERMISSION
IS A SURE FIRE WAY TO FAIL

And one thing I have discovered is when everyone says you're out of your mind, you just might be on to something.

– Jeff Arch, director Sleepless in Seattle

Nope, your eyes aren't deceiving you: I am in fact quoting the director of Sleepless in Seattle, arguably one of the greatest estrogen-inducing movies of all time and second only to Dirty Dancing. (In fact, Dirty Dancing so increased the late Patrick Swayze's estrogen levels he had to make Roadhouse and Point Break to get his testosterone back online).

In Malcolm Gladwell's excellent book, The Tipping Point, he examines how people wait for permission before taking action. Now, what Gladwell means isn't explicit permission, such as a project green light from your superior at work, but the implicit permissions we're exposed to each day. For example, you're a pedestrian at a traffic light and the person next to you decides to cross the street before the signal turns green. Without thinking about it, you follow the person across the street. After all, if someone else does it, it's all right. Further, if you do get in trouble at least you won't be alone. In a previous business venture, I used to put up fliers with "pull tabs"; pull-tabs are little strips of paper containing contact info that can be pulled off the flier. I discovered the response rate was much higher when I displayed fliers with a few tabs already pulled off than with fliers with all tabs intact. Why? Because people wait for permission from others. In most areas in life, no one wants to be first.

From an early age, most of us are conditioned to ask permission before doing anything. This behavior is continually reinforced over the years and most people spend even their adult lives either consciously (but mostly unconsciously) awaiting permission from others. Hell, I know men who refer to their wives as "She Who Must Be Obeyed". These men want someone to pick up where their mothers left off in giving them permission to live their lives. Somehow, many people take comfort in this - as long as someone else thinks it's okay, it must be fine. There's a sense of safety people find in letting others think for them: in relinquishing responsibility for your life you're no longer responsible for success or failure. Well, it looks lame on paper and it's worse in real life - such behavior is acceptable for children but absolutely unacceptable for adults.

When I was a kid I thought adults had it together and took charge of their own lives. As I've gotten older, it's become clear that most adults are over-sized children still seeking approval and permission and waiting for others to tell them what to do, not to mention relinquishing responsibility whenever possible. I read about children far more mature than typical adults and one striking example is Maia, the daughter of one of my online clients. Maia read about a non-profit organization, Elephant Sanctuary on my site. Well, Maia loves all animals, especially elephants, and was inspired by this organization to raise money for their elephants. For her birthday, in lieu of buying gifts, she asked all her friends to make donations to Elephant Sanctuary and raised $500.00. Maia's only ten years old! I, for one, am impressed.

With so much to be gained from freethinking and risk-taking, why are so many adults still permission addicts? The permission payoff is feeling safe and comfortable: you're part of the herd and have support within the collective. If you take the independent path you'll likely have shots fired at you at some point and you'll stand alone in taking the flak. Still, the downside of permission addiction is living a life of quiet desperation. There's no excitement in waiting for others' permission. There's no excitement in following others' example instead of carving your own path - or at least putting your own twist on things.

I think most permission addicts are aware of this and look for tiny outlets of independence and rebellion whenever possible. For example, when I worked in the business development world and traveled with co-workers, I noticed the married men were always desperate to go to strip clubs. The second the business meetings were over, the new mission was finding a strip club.

Now I'm not talking about casual desire as in, "Hey, let's go kill some time and hit a strip club,"

No, I'm talking about compulsion: "We've got to get to a strip club because without my strip-fix this entire trip is a failure! We've got to go now! Where is it, where is it - we've got to find it - arghhhhhhh!"

I don't think visiting strip clubs is any big deal but these guys weren't going to clubs to simply check out the ladies, they were craving that fleeting experience of independence. They were doing something for which they hadn't gotten permission and it excited them. If they'd had their wives' permission - or better yet, their encouragement, they'd unlikely have any desire to go to strip bars, since the fun would be gone.

What separates the successful from the unsuccessful is this: successful people neither wait for permission nor for others to carve a path to follow. Successful people aren't afraid of looking crazy, since who cares what permission-addicts think anyway? Innovative people come up with ideas, think them through, and then follow up with strong action. Waiting around for permission is like waiting around for inspiration...what if no one ever shows up? Why don't you be the first to give it a shot?

THE TIMING IS NEVER PERFECT

For all of the most important things, the timing always sucks. Waiting for a good time to quit your job? The stars will never align and the traffic lights of life will never all be green at the same time.

- Timothy Ferris, The 4-Hour Workweek

I agree with Timothy Ferris that perfect timing to take action doesn't exist. There's always an excuse to put off change and the timing excuse is one of the most effective forms of active procrastination. When other excuses fall short, you can always say the timing isn't right. Ready to quit your lame job? You hate it, but the timing's never right, so you make the best of your two-hour commute by listening to Tony Robbins' Personal Power, and when you complete his program maybe you'll be pumped up enough too quit...at least you hope so. Ready to lose some fat and get strong and healthy? Nah, not yet, though you're barely able to climb stairs, you can always take the elevator, so it's not a priority. Maybe you'll look into getting fit after your first heart attack. Indeed, the timing excuse covers everything and is the most popular resistance tool to change.

As much as the timing excuse is abused, it's overly simplistic to think now is always the time to act, in spite of what's going on in your life - it's a little more complicated than that. Besides, if you're not in the mindset to take action and create major change you won't finish whatever you start; enthusiasm wanes and you can fall right back to where you were. So, yes, there is favorable timing to create change and reduce chance of failure.

How do you know when it's time to create a major change? When the thought of things staying the same makes you sick to your stomach. After you make a change and the inevitable roadblocks come your way, your natural desire is to go back to the way things were. As humans, we seek the path of least resistance and cling to the familiar - no matter how lame it might be - but if the thought of going back sickens you, you'll stay the course. In my previous newsletters, I've described how I felt when I ran into obstacles during the first year of my training business. While things were very tough, the notion of going back to the dotcom world as a business development manager was worse and gave me the impetus to continue. Contemplating working for someone else doing unrewarding work nauseated me. This was a clear sign indicating I was on the right track and as a result I was prepared to do the necessary work to make my business successful.

The bottom line? You have to be fed up with the way things are. Not slightly dissatisfied, or irritated, but completely fed up! Many people avoid getting to this point by playing the distraction game: instead of taking the time to think about what you really want, have a few drinks or watch several hours of TV; put in longer hours at work and spend the weekends digging up the yard and doing home maintenance. Basically, become too busy to notice your dissatisfaction. The distraction game is insidious and can be played all the way to your deathbed. It might be better to put your life on pause and figure out which direction you want to go.

In addition to the physiological signs that you need to make change, the mental side of the equation needs to be addressed. Sometimes you need to know you've covered every angle before you're mentally ready to move forward, otherwise you'll always look back and wonder if you really gave it your all. In a previous business, I tried everything to make my business work: I handed out thousands of business cards and put up fliers and signs on telephone polls all over town. I used surveys, newspaper ads, tons of other things, and finally, mail-order marketing. I was fed up with this business before I tried mail-order marketing and, in fact, I was ready to quit. Then, a good friend of mine, also in the business, told me of a new mail-order marketing method he was working on. As much as I wanted out of the business, I still had to try his strategy, more to clear my conscience than anything else. Of course it didn't work out, which ended up being a good thing, but I knew with complete certainty I'd given everything I had and it wasn't going to work. While some might find such cognizance depressing, to me it was liberating: I knew once and for all this business wasn't for me. This critical realization needs to come forth before productive change takes place. If I'd quit before perceiving this, I'd probably still be wondering if I couldn't have done something different to make it work. This kind of reminiscing wastes time, preventing you from taking advantage of the present. Sometimes you need to get something completely out of your system before moving on with a clear conscience.

Another mental obstacle to overcome is thinking you've failed when you quit something. From early on we're instructed not to be quitters. While this, in spirit, is commendable, the reality is that many things are worth quitting. If you start a new job and hate it after a month, why stick around for a year? If a new relationship bogs down within a few months, will it improve in a year? If your training program requires a lot of time and work yet you only get weaker, do you really think you'll see a turnaround by sticking it out? Being quit-adverse also relinquishes responsibility to others. For example, instead of quitting the job you hate, wait to be fired so you can finally pursue your desired career. Or, instead of breaking up your habitual relationship, wait for your partner to do it, even though you wanted to move out - and on - a long time ago. Quitting isn't always bad, and may be exactly what's needed in order to move forward, but you'll need to get over any guilt feelings that come with it.

When they can no longer recycle excuses regarding perfect timing, people will create bad timing. Blowing money unnecessarily works well: buy a new car, maybe a flat-screen TV, then take an expensive vacation and you'll no longer have any financial reserve, which means fewer options. Make no mistake: money provides options and the ability to take greater financial risk. But now you can't quit your wretched job since you need the money! The bottom line? Our behavior determines our outcome: if you're not prepared to sacrifice, you're not prepared to make major changes. You're simply not ready and perhaps you'll never be ready. Change doesn't take place just when you think it's a nice idea - you have to make it happen, or it happens to you.

There's no "perfect" time to do any important thing in life, but there are indicators that you're ready for change and ready to advance on your goals with a clear conscience. Don't distract yourself from life or allow yourself to get fed up with external circumstances in order to make the changes you can stick with. Get over the idea that being a quitter is synonymous with being a loser and you'll save yourself time and energy. Finally, before attempting to make any major change, ask yourself - what's the worst that can happen? If you can deal with the answer, then what's holding you back?

Is Happiness
Determined By Our Genetics?

Several years ago on a business trip to Dallas I read an interesting article in, of all places, US Airways magazine. The author, Liz Seymour, wrote on the topic of happiness. I expected a patronizing bit about forced positive thinking providing the key to happiness but, to my pleasant surprise, Seymour's article turned out to be the most fascinating I've read in a long time.

How do we define happiness? According to Ed Diener, Professor of Psychology at the University of Illinois, happiness is a combination of "life satisfaction, positive emotions, and low levels of negative emotions." In other words, people who are happy genuinely enjoy their lives and genuinely feel good most of the time. Notice I'm using the word genuinely to distinguish people who are happy from those who merely think happy thoughts - there's a big difference. People who force positive thinking are faking, while happy people are naturally positive: they see the world as full of opportunities rather than fear and sorrow. I'm sure the women reading this agree there's a big difference between genuinely feeling it...and faking it. No need to elaborate further, at least I hope not.

We all have the pursuit of happiness as our goal. At the end of the day every goal we pursue reinforces this end goal of becoming happier: we want to make more money because we think it will make us happier; we want to find a life partner and get married because we think it will make us happier; we want to lose fat and look better because we think it will make us happier. We've been sold a bill of goods that happiness comes from changing external conditions. Unfortunately, achieving real happiness is more complicated than simply changing the externals. According to Seymour, "...happiness is determined by a combination of genetic set points, conditions, and voluntary activities."

Let's start by looking at genetic set points: yes, like other talents, such as intelligence and athletic prowess, a happy disposition can be genetically predetermined. A genetic set point is a factor involved with being happy. Just as some people easily learn calculus, or have a natural ability to run fast, some people find it easy to be happy. On the other hand, just as some people have a hard time learning mathematics or participating in sports, some people have a hard time being happy. For these people happiness takes an effort, just like the effort of academics, or getting in shape, while those with luckier genes may be happier, stay in shape easier, and get better grades. So, if you're miserable, feel free to blame your parents for your lame genetics - and better luck next time!

Lame joking aside, I find the genetic factor in happiness very interesting since I'd never thought of happiness as something genetically determined. How much of a role do genetics play in our happiness? According to studies, genes determine fifty percent of our proclivity for happiness - or for melancholy. While this doesn't mean you'll be doomed to a life of misery and despair if you weren't blessed with happy genes, it does mean you'll have to work harder to achieve happiness. Yes, it's unfair, but you already know life is unfair - after all, the last season of my favorite show, 24, was lame, and if life were fair it would've been excellent, making me a happy camper. Instead, it was lame and I've been miserable ever since. Oh well, at least the last season of my other favorite show, The Shield, was pretty good. So, can I blame my feelings on my genetic set point? No.

While our individual genetic set points play a tremendous role in whether we're happy or not, they're not the only factor. Conditions do play a role but, according to studies, not as big a role as we've been led to believe: conditions make up about eight to fifteen percent of happiness. Thus, if you think you're depressed because you still rent, have a few pounds to lose, or aren't as strong as you'd like to be...think again. Liz Seymour writes, "...variables such as age, education, health, income, personal appearance, and even climate are ineffective at overriding our genetically determined set point." In other words, if your genetic set point favors misery, making a lot of money or even getting a rock hard body won't tip the happiness scales in your favor. Sure, you may temporarily feel better following an achievement or gaining some material possession, such as a house, but within a year you'll be back where you were before the changes occurred.

Ironically, most of us spend our lives trying to change conditions in order to be happy, never realizing why it's not working. Some of you may find this stuff hard to believe, after all, how could one not be happier after becoming a millionaire? Moreover, how could someone who is happy not become miserable after suffering a terrible disease? According to Seymour, studies of lottery winners, on one hand, and people who became paraplegic from an accident, on the other, show clearly that both groups returned to their previous level of happiness within less than a year. In other words: if you're already miserable, your misery will continue even if you become a millionaire but if you're happy in general, even upon becoming a paraplegic, you'll eventually return to happiness after an adaptation phase. The old saying, that people do not change, is truer than we think.

This is why it's difficult to achieve happiness via changing external conditions. Our brains are good at adapting to situations, good or bad. This isn't so hard to understand, think of any important goal you've achieved - remember how anti-climactic it felt? This is the problem with being overly attached to end results: we place too much pressure on achievement changing our mindset. When I first got into weight training, I used to dream about being able to bench press 315 pounds; though eventually I worked up to bench-pressing

315 for seven reps - how did I feel? Great...for a while, then I adapted and returned to the same mindset I had before my strength gain. The much-anticipated change that came with the achievement of my goal didn't last. Eventually, like everyone else, I wanted more.

Of course, no achievement will ever be enough, which is why people unconsciously stay in the anticipation phase and avoid achieving their goals. The anticipation phase is like being a child on the night before Christmas: fantasizing about all the wonderful gifts you'll receive brings more pleasure than the actual experience of opening your gifts. Unfortunately, remaining in the anticipation phase is delusional and won't bring about real happiness; if nothing else, it'll get old and no longer carry the same level of pleasure.

Does this mean we shouldn't bother with goals? Of course not! Goal-less-ness is the path of the cop out. People who claim that everything is illusion are unmotivated people looking to avoid growth and change. The key is setting goals and achieving them for the sake of doing it. As mentioned earlier, according to the ancient Hindu text, The Bhagavad Gita, we've a right to our actions but not the results of those actions: our reward is the process and experience rather than any form of attainment. Goal achievements are road signs that we're heading in the right direction and ready to grow into our next phase. Without achieving goals, we're doomed to repeating our same experiences over and over again. According to John Elliot, author of The New Science Of Working Less To Accomplish More, we perform better when we're fully in the moment and unattached to outcome: life's fullest moments can be reduced to those moments in which we're fully present with no thoughts of past or future. These are the moments in which we're fully alive and time seems to stand still. Clearly, enjoying life moment-to-moment, rather than persisting with fearful thoughts, enhances our genetic set points.

Everyone wants to be happy whether they realize it or not and even if they don't want to admit it. We need to realize that happiness isn't a result of focusing on conditions. We need to focus on enhancing our genetic set points in order to stack the odds of personal happiness in our favor. If you're not happy making $50,000 you won't be happy making $250,000: the problem is within our minds, not external conditions.

Fortunately, we don't have to lie back and accept the genetic set point we've been dealt. Just as anyone can get smarter and build stronger muscles, so can we develop stronger genetic set points for happiness. Seymour writes that one option is taking drugs - after all, we're a pill-popping society and there exist pills for every problem under the sun, including a poor outlook on life. Selective serotonin re-uptake inhibitors, such as Prozac and Zoloft, prolong the action of serotonin in the brain. Serotonin is a chemical that's helpful with mood and is adequately produced by people who are naturally happy. For people with chemical imbalances, I can see how these drugs are a godsend. Some people really benefit from these drugs or by supplementing the amino acids tyrosine and tryptophan, which create serotonin in the brain. However, taking drugs or even nutritional supplements isn't a solution for everyone. In fact, taking such drugs may be a way of avoiding the problem: our actions must lead to sustained improvements, not drug dependence.

If not drugs, then what? One, we need to learn to better handle stress. People with natural stress management skills are inevitably happier. As hard as it is to fathom, a soldier in Iraq under a hail of bullets may be less stressed than your average Los Angeles millionaire complaining about an overcooked steak...if the former has superior stress-management skills and thus a greater genetic "happiness" set point.

What about the people who don't have a natural stress-management ability? Fortunately, there's hope for stress-management under-achievers. According to Seymour, one method proven to be effective at increasing set-point happiness is a daily meditation practice. According to researchers at the Laboratory For Affective Neuroscience at the University of Wisconsin, meditation stimulates the brain's left pre-frontal cortex. This is the part of the brain most active when we're happy and alert, so meditation is very effective at lowering stress and increasing feelings of happiness. Maybe this is why Buddhist monks seem to smile so much? It can't have anything to do with eating beans and rice everyday and abstaining from sex! Otherwise, my advice is to quit your job, shave your head and move into your local temple - just kidding (well, not the part about quitting your job!)

We can stay in this world and become happier: merely devote some time to meditation and stimulate the left pre-frontal cortex. Of course, this is easier said than done for those of us not jumping for joy like a bunch of idiots. People find meditation difficult, and I'm no exception. Fortunately, there are meditation programs that work for those us who under-achieve at stimulating the left pre-frontal cortex while chanting and sitting in the lotus position. My favorite meditation program is Holosync. Read about it at the end of this article.

Seymour mentions another method useful for steering our set points toward the world of happiness: cognitive therapy. Cognitive therapy works by teaching us how to recognize negative patterns and breaking them. Instead of dwelling on the negative, cognitive therapy teaches us to focus on the thought patterns which make us happy. Even miserable people have their happy moments. The key is to develop the happy moments and avoid bogging down in misery ruts.

Some of you are thinking that cognitive therapy is "positive thinking" mumbo-jumbo but really it isn't. With positive thinking, you're in denial: rather than accepting the fact that some things are, in fact, negative, you're taught to spin every situation into a positive - no matter what. The problem is we unconsciously know we're lying to ourselves and don't really buy it. Positive thinking devotees are paranoid of any negative thought and feel guilty when such thoughts arise - neither healthy nor realistic.

Faking happiness isn't the same as authentic happiness. With cognitive therapy, you learn to break negative patterns by listening to feedback - sounds complicated right? It isn't. Here's an example:

you watch two hours of television news and get bombarded with all the problems in the world - how do you feel afterwards? Similar to millions of other people: you feel depressed and powerless. These feelings stay with you for the rest of the day - or even week - and are compounded every time you watch the news. What should you do? Well, stop watching the news! What value is it providing you? Are you doing anything positive with the information? If no, then stop your source of negativity. Or, get empowered and do something about it. For example, if you see a news segment on kids who've been victimized, why not join an organization that helps abused kids? When you empower yourself, you can transform negative energy into a positive outcome. Empowered actions are gratifying and bring us longer lasting happiness than such simple pleasures as eating dessert or watching a good movie.

Cognitive therapy teaches us how things affect us - whether positive or negative. Here's another example: you see an injured animal on the side of the road but instead of driving by muttering how terrible it is, you pull over, wrap the wounded animal in a towel and take it to a vet. Because of this compassionate act the animal makes a full recovery and you feel like a million bucks all week. Of course the feeling will eventually wear off, but you can prolong it or invite it back by putting in some volunteer hours at an animal shelter or other reputable non-profit organization for animals. Again, you're taking the path of empowerment, and when we're empowered, we're unstressed and happy. When we play a role in improving the world around us, we're gratified and, again, actions resulting in gratification provide longer periods of happiness.

What about seeking out those activities in which we obtain pleasure? Well, if we focus on our pleasure more often, we're less likely to experience depression. Terrific! Unfortunately, according to Seymour, studies show that such pleasures are fleeting in nature. For example, great sex is great - for a while - but the feeling eventually wears off until your next sex fix. All you create with sex in such a situation is another compulsion, also known as a distraction. Now

I'm the last person to knock sex in any way and I'm not saying sex is a waste of your time! A strong sex drive is a strong sign of health and vitality but don't deceive yourself that sexual pleasure is a solution for creating permanent change when your set point is turned towards sorrow.

Pleasures are a great and important aspect of life but gratifications bring longer lasting happiness. Seymour writes, "...gratifications are activities that call on our skills and strengths and give us a sense of a job well done." Personally, I enjoy pleasure more when the gratifications are in full effect. Pleasure is like icing on the cake: while the icing is part of enjoying cake, it can't replace the cake. A personal example to drive this point home: several years ago I did a kettlebell workshop with my good friend Dylan Thomas in NYC. The workshop was looking disastrous: I had to change the venue three times, as booked venues kept falling though. Then, a guy who was supposed to present the workshop with me had to bail out just days before the event. With this news, I had several people cancel right off the bat and several more express anger via email, accusing me of lacking professionalism. It also seemed the people still planning on coming weren't bringing their positive vibes: many were pissed off and told me they'd have canceled but for their non-refundable airfares. The workshop foreboded disaster and I knew it had to be the best of my career to turn things around.

To make a long story short: Dylan and I put on a great workshop and everyone left happy. In fact, it turned out to be one of the most enthusiastic groups I've ever worked with and everyone had a blast. Instead of getting depressed about everything going wrong, we empowered ourselves by taking charge of what we could and at the end of the day that was enough and it all worked out.

I received immense gratification from pulling off that workshop. It was a great group, a fun day, and afterwards a few of us went out for a few too many drinks. We had a blast...until the next day's arrival of hell's hangover. Where am I going with this? The pleasure of going out and having some fun on the town was that much sweeter due to the gratification of that workshop's success. If we'd simply traveled to NYC and had a night out, it wouldn't have been anywhere near as sweet or meaningful.

A night of pleasure lasts a night but a day of gratification can last a lifetime. We need to focus on developing opportunities for gratification - and thus long lasting happiness - rather than pursuing those fleeting pleasures. My own rule of thumb is: enjoy pleasures but focus on gratifications.

While the art of happiness may not be an easy craft to develop and master but one at which we must work hard - just like any goal in life - it's probably the most important goal we can achieve. After all, what else matters if you don't find happiness in this life? Don't be a slave to your genetic set point - anything can be improved. Just as you can learn more and become more intelligent - or lift more and get stronger - you're capable of greater, more meaningful, happiness. Even if you never win the award for Happiest Person on the Planet, deepening your experience of happiness is reward enough. Dedicate your life to creating plentiful opportunities for gratification and enjoying pleasurable activities and improve your stress-management skills - this is what living life aggressively is all about.

Is Happiness Determined
By Our Genetics? Part Two

You're happiest while you're making the greatest contribution
                                                    — *Robert Kennedy*

It's an interesting notion that so much of our happiness is genetically based. While genetics may be a large factor for most people, I find it hard to believe that it's responsible for 50% of happiness - or sadness - across the board. I find it hard to believe that changing conditions only amounts to 8-15% of happiness for everyone. Upon what am I basing this? Myself of course! Now is the time for another personal story.

While I'm not a depressive person by nature, I've gone through periods in my life wherein I was greatly unsatisfied. These times were always condition-based and always took place during times in which I wasn't taking charge of my life and I wasn't doing anything gratifying. Additionally, being in the wrong relationship is stressful and depressing.

When you dread going home to deal with your significant other, it's a sign you're with the wrong person. We human beings are highly adaptive organisms, which can lead us to dealing with lame situations instead of doing something to provoke major - positive - changes. Fortunately for me, I hate comfort zones and will only stay in them for so long. Inevitably, I reach a tipping point in which I make major changes leading to a greater level of happiness. Without question, when I changed from dissatisfying work and relationships, my happiness increased. Why wouldn't it? What we do for a living, and whom we spend time with, impacts our life and it's hard to be happy in a job you hate or around people who drain you.

I'm much happier now than when I worked for other people. I set my own hours, spontaneously take a day or a week off, spend more time with friends and family and - most importantly - there's a lot of gratification in what I do and I feel good knowing I make a positive difference in the lives of others. One of the things about my business I most enjoy is putting out my online magazine, which isn't something for which I get paid. Of course, the objective of my online magazine is to generate income, but thousands of people benefit from each issue without ever spending a dime on my business and I'm fine with that, as long as they don't email me for more free info, since there's a line between gratification and exploitation!

Changing from an unrewarding job wasn't the only big impact on my happiness: I'm also much happier now, with my wife Carol, than in any previous relationship - or when I was single. While I don't hold the illusion that a great relationship makes up for an unrewarding career (or life) it certainly makes life more enjoyable, and a great support system can make all the difference when improving on life's other, messier areas. No matter how much it's genetically set, changing conditions definitely made a big jump in my personal happiness.

I'm not encouraging you to quit your job and start your own business or non-profit organization. I'm encouraging you to apply critical thinking skills to your life and determine what can be done to increase your own happiness. Quitting your job may not be the answer. You might enjoy working for others and hate the idea of working for yourself and there's nothing wrong with that...the last thing I want is for you to quit your job and be left unable to afford my products and services. All joking aside, I'm encouraging you to develop a personalized plan for increasing your happiness, and the more you know about yourself, the more effectively you can develop that plan. You can observe what others are doing and imitate but that's a big mistake, since what works for them (if it even works at all) won't necessarily work for you. Forget what other people think you should do and take on the responsibility of determining what's best for yourself. If you're not prepared to do so, then you're not yet an adult, regardless of your age.

As mentioned earlier, I've noticed I get struck with mild depression when I'm not growing and improving. I'm not talking about financially. Yes, I run a business and want to make more money each year but that's not what I'm taking about. Making more money doesn't increase my level of happiness: I use money as a measure that my business is moving in the right direction and that I'm reaching and helping more people. It also allows me to support organizations that I believe in and enjoy life.

When it comes to growth, I'm taking about personal growth, as in learning more about life and learning more about myself. I like the idea of learning more every year and accomplishing more, compared to repeating the same year twenty times over. Time goes by, whether we want it to or not, and there's no slowing it down. You can either take charge of your life or grow or simply let the years pass by. When I sense the years are passing me by, I feel depression. Being productive and accomplishing goals are major contributors to my happiness. I enjoy relaxing and kicking back...but only for so long. Eventually I need to jump back in the game and do the things, which gratify me.

Now that we've discussed happiness, let's take a look at melancholy. Melancholy can be an organic sign we need to make changes in our lives. If we use improper form while strength training, we'll develop an injury; this is a sign we need to modify form. Melancholy is a sign to stop, assess your life, and evaluate what needs to change. It might not be anything external, such as losing weight or relocating, but may mean you need to begin a meditation practice, or meditate more often to develop a higher tolerance for stress. It may mean that you need to have your hormones, such as testosterone and DHEA, checked, to ensure you're not in a depleted state. Finally, it may mean you need to seek more opportunities for gratification. On the other hand, clinical depression is a more serious problem requiring professional help.

Even if fifty percent of happiness is genetically set, the other fifty percent remains within our power to focus upon and improve. In addition to changing external conditions, such as dead-end relationships and unrewarding work, we need to maximize our health potential by optimizing our hormones, reducing stress, and increasing stress-management skills.

As I mentioned in the last chapter, meditation is a proven method of reducing cortisol and should be practiced daily. You don't have to sit in the lotus position chanting for an hour, you might instead incorporate daily walks while focusing on the breath, all of which works to increase levels of epinephrine, a mood-boosting hormone. Other forms of active meditation are qi gong and tai chi. Discover what's a good fit for you and practice it regularly.

Regular physical exercise is a popular method of reducing cortisol levels and increasing stress-management reserves but, when taken too far, exercise becomes a negative activity, resulting in an increase in cortisol, anxiety, weakened immunity, and poor mood from the decrease in "good feeling" hormones. Training is a medicine: in order to be effective, the dose must be precise. Avoid being a training/stimulus addict and follow planned, efficient programs matching your goals and lifestyle.

An interesting way to reduce cortisol levels is avoiding clutter! My brother told me about an interesting article discussing a connection between having a messy environment and increased cortisol levels. It's difficult to maintain a clear and focused mind within the middle of a mess! Donate the clothes you never wear to the local Goodwill or Salvation Army and stop buying junk to fill your internal void - it won't work. If you're addicted to buying things, go to your local children's hospital and ask a bunch of kids what they want, then get to work. I promise, buying them things will be more gratifying than adding more junk to your own environment.

Much of self-imposed misery comes from over reliance on the approval of others. Get over your need for approval and validation and pursue your goals for their own sake and for your own excellence. Praise is fleeting and it's certain that most people from whom you seek validation are more insecure than yourself!

Finally, while money doesn't buy happiness, financial stress can certainly reduce your happiness. I've been in debt more than once and you can believe I'm much happier debt-free. You're not free when you owe money and I'm amazed how casual people are about immense credit card debts. People are willing to go into tremendous debt to mimic the American dream, which isn't authentic if it's not earned and acquired on your own terms. Living a pretense is unconsciously stressful: while money won't buy happiness, it can negotiate peace of mind. Believe me, if your loved one needs an expensive operation, you'll be much happier paying for the operation than bearing the stress bombardment that comes with lack.

For some people, happiness is a birthright; for many of us it's an elusive potential. Certainly, just as we train to get stronger and smarter, we must train to become happier. I wish you smooth sailing with your happiness-training program.

Stop Complaining and Take Charge of Your Life

I was discovering that life just simply isn't fair, but the difference emerges among the people that accept that idea--embrace it even--and bask in the unsung glory of knowing that each obstacle overcome along the way only adds to the satisfaction in the end. Nothing great, after all, was ever accomplished by anyone sulking in his or her misery.

          ---Adam Shepard, author of Scratch Beginnings

In his provocative book, Scratch Beginnings: Me, $25, and the Search for the American Dream, Adam Shepard undertakes a year-long experiment to ascertain first-hand the state of the American Dream. Challenging himself to start with next-to-nothing, and within a year's time accrue $2500.00 in savings, live in a furnished apartment (solo or with roommate) and possess a vehicle, Adam travels out of state, where he has no contacts, arriving with only $25.00 and the clothes on his back. Within ten months, Adam has met his stated goals and exceeded his own expectations by saving $5000.00. He achieves this without help from friends, family or the credit card he keeps in his pocket for emergencies. Further, when applying for jobs, he never discloses he is a college graduate. A crucial ingredient to Adam's success is his lack of self-pity: he is instead occupied in taking action to reach his objectives. This is a trait you will always see with successful people.

  Adam's journey starts in Charleston, South Carolina, where, with $25.00 in his pocket, the first roof over his head is the local homeless shelter. From this humble base (and with the help of food stamps) he takes on any job offered. Breaking with the current social norm, Adam cheerfully accepts as fact that when you have nothing, no job is beneath you, and from cleaning up dog crap in backyards in summer heat to every other form of day labor he works from sunrise to sunset. Adam firmly applies his work ethic to his goal of leaving the shelter as soon as possible. He considers any job better than sitting around and by working an odd assortment of jobs, creates a forward momentum, eventually getting hired by a moving company at a starting rate of $7.00 an hour, which, over time, grows to ten dollars an hour, enabling him to vacate the homeless shelter and progress to a shared apartment. After observing other shelter residents prematurely leave, only to end up back in the shelter again when hit with unanticipated expenses, Adam pointedly remains at the shelter until he's saved up adequate funds all the while maintaining an extremely frugal life style, scrimping every dollar possible i.e. neither restaurant meals nor vacations, and all clothing purchases are second-hand. Adam's imperative to leave the homeless shelter is tendered with patience, as well as the sacrifices necessary to ensure that once he gets out he'll stay out.

Adam understands that which many people miss: forward movement often requires personal sacrifice - or, you can't have it all, all the time. Such choices may bring about phases in your life which are out of balance, e.g. you might even have to work seven days a week, and not only without a vacation, but going to bed each night wiped out from the day's work, all the while saving every dollar possible and delaying all your favorite gratifications. However, you'd be surprised what you can make happen in just a year of deliberate and focused work. Later, once things get going, you can ease up on the reins and into a more balanced, and comfortable lifestyle.

Adam encounters all sorts of people throughout his journey. There are some content with living and hanging out at the shelter all day, while others have ended up at the shelter with more ambition, forming determined plans to get back on their feet and depart the shelter circuit. He notices this second group don't blame anyone else for their circumstances, but accept full accountability, bolster it with a solid work ethic and a vision of where they want to be - and how to get there.

Scratch Beginnings is a rebuttal to (and rejection of) Nickel and Dimed, journalist Barbara Ehrenreich's undercover investigative account on whether the so-called "working poor" could survive on minimum wage employment. Over the course of several months, Ehrenreich hired on as waitress, Wal-Mart associate, nursing home assistant, and franchise service house maid, concluding that holding a single minimum wage job was insufficient for reasonable subsistence. What Barbara failed to realize is that increasing the minimum wage will drive up the price of everything else and people will be right back where they started. In paying higher wages to workers, employers will, in turn, charge more for products and services. The question is not whether people can subsist on the minimum wage, but why would anyone settle for a subsistence lifestyle? If you have to start out there, fine, I respect anyone who works over those who would mooch off others. But why stay at a minimum wage job? People can do better than that and should strive to do so. In fact, in a labor market, minimum wage jobs are supposed to be terrible - this motivates people to accumulate relevant skills. I worked a few minimum wage jobs in my previous life and never in my mind did I consider staying at any of them. In our current economic retraction, I hear more bitching from people than ever. People complain about the difficulties of the job market and how the government isn't helping them enough. While there may be some truth to this, I never hear these same people bitching about their own complicity in this mess. This doesn't surprise me, as blaming others, and circumstances, is a common denominator among the unsuccessful.

Find yourself in a predicament? Instead of blaming others, why not take the time to make an honest self-assessment? If you are willing to be this ruthless with yourself, of understanding why you are where you are at this point in time, then you will be able to move forward from here. Clarity may not always be pleasant but there is beauty in the truth and, often, dramatic life changes can result.

The single thing you have control over is this: what are you prepared to do now? Are you content with blaming others, effectively avoiding progression, and ensuring your continuing plummet into mediocrity and irrelevance? Or are you prepared to take responsibility for your life and focus on your potential?

In my experience, moving forward requires your becoming completely fed up and disgusted with yourself, otherwise it's easier to give up and blame others when things get tough. People who give up at the first roadblock were never serious about the goal in the first place. Perhaps it sounded good or someone else recommended it to them. In contrast, when there's a real commitment, roadblocks are simply obstacles to blast though on the way to the goal. They are not only expected but overcome with full force and no regrets.

A good friend of mine always claimed to want his own business but the timing was never right. Then, one day he went to the office and was overcome by nausea. The idea of even one more day at that job caused him to feel sick to his stomach - a sure-fire sign he was ready to move on. The state of being completely fed up with yourself and your circumstances means you are ready to move on and push forward with full commitment. Pursuing a goal with an ambivalent or cavalier attitude is a red flag for ensuing failure.

Occasionally, people tell me that if their entrepreneurial pursuit fails to bear fruit, they'll just return to their old job. I tell them to give up now, since they lack sincerity in their effort. At such times, the last thing on your mind should be visions of your plans not working out. Focus so intently upon what it is you intend to achieve that such thoughts never enter the mind. That sort of negative reality only serves those people who strive for mediocrity, not those who wish to see positive - and dramatic - outcomes to their dreams.

Life seems not always fair, no doubt. Everyone encounters problems, ranging from the inconvenient to the immense, yet ultimately each of us must take individual charge of our lives. As long as you remain focused upon what others should be doing for you (i.e. the past), you cannot move forward into the future. This is the realm of the loser. Winners are too focused on what they can do - and are too busy doing it - to concern themselves with circumstances.

WHAT ARE YOU
PREPARED TO DO NOW?

After all is said and done, more is said than done

– Aesop

I cannot think of a better way to end my book than to draw upon two of my favorite movies of all time, The Untouchables and Star Trek III. Lets start with The Untouchables. This classic hit the theatres in 1986, and stars Kevin Costner, Sean Connery, Andy Garcia, and Robert DeNiro. It takes place during the prohibition era, and is a dramatic adaptation of Elliot Ness' takedown of Al Capone. While that is the backdrop, the movie is far more than a gangster movie and is really about the evolution of Elliot Ness, played by Kevin Costner. I was thirteen when I first saw this movie and I loved it then. However, each time I see it I love it even more, as I am a different person each time. There is so much depth in the movie and so many life lessons to learn. It also has some of the best lines of all time. If you have not seen it, you need to rent it today.

In the beginning of the movie Elliot Ness starts off as a play by the rules prohibitionist official. He wants to take down the gangster Al Capone, played immaculately by Robert DeNiro, but is not willing to break any rules. He wants to do it by the book. After failing to make any headway, Elliot goes for a late night walk and meets an experienced and street-smart cop named Malone, played masterfully by Sean Connery. One gets the impression that Malone used to be a cop that wanted to make a difference, but is now jaded and spends his evenings walking the beat and keeping a low profile. Elliot sees something in Malone and has an epiphany. Elliot realizes that he needs to think outside the box and recruit a cop that understands how things get done in Chicago; a man that has the experience, wisdom, and connections to make things happen.

Elliot attempts to recruit Malone but Malone initially resists. He realizes all too well what needs to be done to take down Capone and does not want to put himself in harms way. However, after much deliberation and feelings of shame for being a coward, Malone agrees to help Elliot and essentially becomes his mentor. No longer the man that does not want to rock the boat, Malone is now the man that guides Elliot and helps him to evolve.

In a pivotal scene, Malone asks Elliot what he is prepared to do to take down Capone. Elliot responds that he is willing to do everything within the law. Malone retorts by asking Elliot what he is prepared to do beyond the law. Malone makes it clear that you cannot beat an opponent that does not have any rules constricting their actions. If you want to take down such an opponent, you have to understand them clearly and also understand yourself fully and be honest with how far you are willing to take it. Just as in life, if you have not taken the time to do the self-inventory to know yourself, then you are doomed. You may go on to make lots of money and achieve some other goals, but you will never be truly self realized which is what real success is all about. You will be an empty hollow being.

Elliot initially resists becoming the man he despises, but he eventually realizes that if he wants to take down Capone, he has to be willing to go into dark territory and use that energy against Capone. We all have dark energy and light energy, and we need to have the courage to tap into both for the full experience of life, and to evolve fully. At one point in the movie Ness admits that he has broken many laws that he swore to uphold and that he despises many of the things he has done. But, at the end of the day he feels just, as it is what had to be done, for what he feels is the greater good.

In a very powerful scene in the movie, Elliot finds Malone mortally wounded. Malone musters up all of the energy he can to tell Elliot what his next move needs to be. With his last breath he pulls Elliot close and emphatically says, "What are you prepared to do?" This is a question you need to ask yourself and then be honest with the answer before you go after any goal. Failure to do so will take you to terrible places you never dreamed possible, and the consequences can be disastrous.

The next scene after Malone's death shows clearly that Elliot is prepared to go all the way, and eventually he takes down Al Capone. In the beginning of the movie Elliot does not know himself, and as a result keeps losing to the superior opponent of Al Capone. By the end of the movie, Elliot knows exactly who he is and beats Capone at his own game. He also understands what loyalty is and what it means to be a real friend. In another incredible scene, Capone's henchman admits that he killed Malone and that Malone died like a coward. Elliot Ness grabs the henchman and throws him off a building and watches him fall to his death. Forget the rules, this scumbag killed Elliot's friend; a friend that gave him the guidance to take down Capone; a friend that gave his life to further Elliot's cause; a friend that helped Ness evolve and become the man he needed to become. The bonds that we make with others in this world are important and there is no amount of money that will buy back broken bonds. Once you have sold yourself out, or those that put their trust in you, you have sold your soul. That brings me to one of my other favorite movies: Start Trek III: The Search For Spock.

Yes I am a Star Trek fan but only of the real Stark Trek with Captain Kirk, McCoy, and Spock. Forget about all the other politically correct Start Trek shows and movies which were all as boring as building an ant farm. For those of you that are not Star Trek fans, Star Trek III picks up immediately after the events in Star Trek II. In Start Trek II, Kirk's best friend Spock sacrifices himself to save the crew. His last words to Kirk are that the needs of the many out weigh the needs of the few, or the one. Kirk is distraught after the loss of his close friend and has a hard time moving on. While he has always been a risk taker and a courageous Captain, he never had to face death until Spock sacrificed himself. He always found a way to turn a losing situation into a winning one until now.

Upon returning home, Spock's father Sarek asks Kirk why he did not bring Spock's body back to his home planet of Vulcan. Kirk responds by saying he saw no reason to, as Spock died back on the Enterprise. Sarek says that only his body died and that his consciousness could have been passed on. He explains to Kirk that Spock would have found a way to pass his consciousness on before passing. Together they determine that Spock did in fact pass his consciousness on to Dr McCoy. McCoy is now in a bipolar state as he essentially has another being's consciousness within. Kirk realizes that he has to return to the planet where he left Spock's body and then bring both McCoy and Spock back to Vulcan to transfer Spock's consciousness. Kirk swears to Sarek that he will do whatever is necessary to make this happen. Of course, Kirk's resolve is about to be tested and that is where the movie gets very interesting.

Kirk tries to get his ship back but his superior refuses to give the Enterprise back to him. Kirk then tries to acquire another ship but again his superior does not allow it. Kirk has to make a choice, follow orders and keep his career or disobey orders and risk his career as well as criminal penalties. Of course there really is no choice. Kirk is a man of integrity that does not sell out his friends. He knows what needs to be done, and puts together a machination to steal the Enterprise and obtain Spock's body. Of course Kirk cannot do it alone and enlists his former crew to help him. The crew has no problem helping Kirk, they have the utmost respect for him. They help him get the Enterprise back and once on board Kirk tells his crew that he and McCoy have to go forward, but that he does not expect everyone else to join them. The last thing he wants to do is get his loyal crew members in trouble. They interrupt Kirk and say they are in and that they are wasting time and need to get going. That is the kind of confidence that a real leader inspires in others. No one is going to be loyal to a jerk CEO that treats employees like crap. However a real leader that is a great person can get others to make sacrifices without even asking.

To make a long story short they successfully retrieve Spock's body and transfer his consciousness from McCoy. However, the success is bittersweet as many sacrifices had to be made. Kirk has to destroy his beloved ship in order to defeat an enemy. As Kirk watches his ship blow up he turns to McCoy and says, "My God Bones what have I done?" McCoy responds, "What you had to do, what you always do, turn death into a chance for life." Kirk always knew what to do when the heat was on. Anyone can make a good decision when the pressure is not on (although few do), but when the pressure is immense you find out who you really are and what you are made of. The ship is not the only sacrifice that occurs along the way. Kirk's son is caught by the enemy and killed when he tries to protect his friends. Like his father he is courageous and prepared to sacrifice for the benefit of others.

Spock's father Sarek is blown away by what Kirk went through to help Spock. Sarek says the cost was too high and Kirk responds by saying that if he never tried the cost would have been his soul. That is the cost for you for not having the courage to aspire to greatness. That is the cost to you for not having the courage to pursue your passion. What you lose is everything. Shakespeare said that a brave man dies but once, but a coward dies many times. A life of quiet desperation is a process of dying a little bit each day.

Many of you may be failing to see the connection between great movies like The Untouchables, Star Trek III, and your own life. Neither story is real so what possible real world application could they have? You are missing the point. Stories are an important component on how we grow in this world. We learn a lot about life through stories. We derive a great deal of inspiration to be better people through stories. We acquire courage and perseverance to push hard and achieve our goals through stories. Yet many fail to see the connection and apply what they learn through stories to their own life. They fail to become the heroes they need to be to save themselves. They watch a movie and then go on with their lives completely unaffected. A great movie or story has the power to leave us a different person. Stories have the power to make us push harder to evolve and learn more about ourselves.

The problem is we far too often play the distraction game. We do not want to think about who we are, to do so is a let down. We are not as courageous as the characters in movies or novels. It is much easier to lead a life of quiet desperation and to simply go with the flow. Such people are never genuinely happy no matter how good they are at lying to themselves. Unfortunately more people are better at lying to themselves then they are at being honest which is the first critical ingredient to ever lasting change and evolution.

This book is about taking charge of your life and having the courage to make your life your message. In the end the truth is in your actions not in what you say. Your life is the most powerful message that you can convey to others. Living your authentic life, is more powerful than any book you may write, or anything you may say.

Life is about facing challenges full on. It is about not being afraid to make mistakes, having the wherewithal to learn from mistakes, and having the courage and resolve to keep pushing forward. It is about living with loss, living with gain, and just flat out living. Not living vicariously through others, or accepting a life that is not your full potential.

You know what you need to do. You do not need to go to a motivational seminar. You do not need to sign up for counseling sessions. You know what you need to do if you are willing to be honest with yourself. Stop lying to yourself and take charge of your life. The timing will never be perfect. The stars are not going to align and carve an easy path for you. Doing more research will not help. Waiting to get approval or a pat from others will not help. You are in the ring of life alone, and you have to fight the good fight and be consumed by the process - that you arrive at the destination without being attached to the goal. The clock is ticking and you are running out of time. Each day you delay is another day wasted. Each day you accept a life of mediocrity is another day wasted.

Will things get easier when you burn your bridges and finally pursue your passion? In some ways yes and in other ways things will get harder, much harder! Why go after your passion if it will make your life harder? Because you will not care that your life is harder. It is what you want to do. You will embrace the adversity and enjoy every minute of it.

The Buddha said that life is suffering and he was right. However, within that suffering is the greatest pleasure of all the opportunity for self-realization. The opportunity to really find out who you are and what you are made of. Until you have faced major challenges you will never be fully self-realized. Until you face death head on you will never truly appreciate your life.

Whatever your passion is. It will be very hard to make it happen. It will take longer than you think and you will suffer along the way. When you do finally make it happen, challenges that you never believed you could handle will come your way, and you know what? You will do just fine. In fact you will enjoy it. When you look back you will miss the challenges and want them back. You will miss the thrill of the day you decided that you deserve more in life and had the courage to finally pursue it and never look back. You will miss rolling up your sleeves and getting your hands dirty.

What do you lose in never trying? Similar to Kirk if you never try the cost will be your soul.

What are you prepared to do now?

REFERENCES

It is time to live life aggressively!

Gandhi, Mahatma. 1993. *Gandhi An Autobiography: The Story of My Experiments With Truth*. Boston, MA.: Beacon Press.

Chapter One

Hofmekler, Ori. 2007. *The Anti-estrogenic Diet*. Berkley, CA.: North Atlantic Books.

Hofmekler, Ori. 2008. *Maximum Muscle, Minimum Fat*. Berkley, CA.: North Atlantic Books.

Richards, Byron. 2009. *Mastering Leptin*. Minneapolis, MN.: Wellness Resources Books.

Sears, Barry. 1998. *The Anti-aging Zone*. New York, NY.: William Morrow.

Chapter Two

Marcinko, Richard. 1997. *Leadership Secrets of the Rogue Warrior*. New York, NY.: Pocket.

Chapter Five

Gilbert, Daniel. 2006. *Stumbling on Happiness*. New York, NY.: Knopf.

Chapter Nine

Pollan, Michael. 2008. *In Defense of Food: An Eater's Manifesto*. New York, NY.: Penguin Press.

Chapter Eleven

Mitchell, Steven. 2000. *Bhagavad Gita: A New Translation*. New York, NY.: Three Rivers Press.

Chapter Twelve

Gladwell, Malcolm. 2008. *Outliers*. New York, NY.: Little Brown And Company.

Chapter Thirteen

Lehrer, Jonah. 2009. *How We Decide*. New York, NY.: HMH Publishing.

Chapter Sixteen

Coyle, Daniel. 2009. *The Talent Code*. New York, NY.: A Bantam Book.
Haley, Alex, Malcolm X. 1987. *The Autobiography of Malcolm X: As Told to Alex Haley*. New York, NY.: Ballantine Books.

Chapter Seventeen

Haley, Alex, Malcolm X. 1987. *The Autobiography of Malcolm X: As Told to Alex Haley*. New York, NY.: Ballantine Books.

Chapter Nineteen

Ariely, Dan. 2008. *Predictably Irrational*. New York, NY.: Harper Collins.

Chapter Twenty

Gallagher, Marty. 2008. *The Purposeful Primitive*. Saint Paul, MN.: Dragondoor Publications.
Hallinan, Joseph T. 2009. *Why We Make Mistakes*. New York, NY.: Broadway Books.

Chapter Twenty-one

Elfinstone, Hugo W. 2007. *Compassionate Honesty*. Frederick, MD.: Publish America.

Chapter Twenty-two

Zimbardo, Philip. 2008. *The Lucifer Effect*. New York, NY.: Random House Trade Paperbacks.

Chapter Twenty-three

Lambert, Kelly. 2008. *Lifting Depression*. New York, NY.: Basic Books.

Chapter Twenty-four

Elliot, John. 2006. *Overachievement: The New Science of Working Less to Accomplish*. New York, NY.: Portfolio Books.

Chapter Twenty-five

Elliot, John. 2006. *Overachievement: The New Science of Working Less to Accomplish*. New York, NY.: Portfolio Books.

Chapter Twenty-six

Fadiman, Frager. 1999. *Essential Sufism*. New York, NY.: HarperOne.
Herbert, Frank. 1990. *Dune*. New York, NY.: Ace Books.

Chapter Twenty-seven

Chu, Chin-Ning. 2000. *Do Less, Achieve More*. New York, NY.: Harper Paperbacks.

Chapter Thirty

Colvin, Geoff. 2008. *Talent Is Overrated*. New York, NY.: Portfolio Hardcover

Chapter Thirty-two

Gladwell, Malcolm. 2002. *The Tipping Point*. New York, NY.: Back Bay Books.

Chapter Thirty-three

Ferris, Timothy. 2007. *The 4-Hour Workweek*. New York, NY.: Crown Publishing Group.

Chapter Thirty-six

Shepherd, Adam. 2007. *Scratch Beginnings*. New York, NY.: SB Press.

Conclusion

Aesop. 1996. *Aesop's Fables*. New York, NY.: Penguin Popular Classics.

AGGRESSIVE STRENGTH RECOMMENDED READING LIST

There are many books that I find thought provoking and this list would go on for 100 pages if I listed every single one. However, I think the following are a great selection that you will enjoy. I recommend all of them highly.

SELF INVENTORY

The following are a list of books that will make a tremendous impact on your business life. In addition, these books will provide some insight on how you and others operate. The more you know about yourself and others the stronger you are.

Lifting Depression by Kelly Lambert, Ph.D

A very interesting book and Dr Lambert does a great job detailing what actually works for battling depression and improving mood. She does a great job conveying the pitfalls of talk therapy and also covers the importance of the sex hormone DHEA for optimal mood. As someone that studies hormone optimization I know how important it is to have optimal levels of DHEA for optimal stress management. The better your stress reserves the better you will feel. I was elated to see Dr Lambert discuss the importance of DHEA as few health professionals are as progressive.

The Talent Code by Daniel Coyle

This is a fascinating look at why talent is overrated. People that are successful are masters because they put in 10,000 hours of concerted effort in their crafts. It is not something they are born with, it is something that is developed through hours and years of focused efforts.

The New Science Of Working Less To Accomplish More by John Elliot, Ph.D

An interesting look at how to use stress and pressure to one's advantage. Stress and pressure makes one sharp and you should not be worried if you feel both before taking on any challenge. In fact you should be worried if you do not feel either.

Why We Make Mistakes by Joe Hallinan

A great look at the reasons why we make mistakes and why we keep making them. Learn why few learn from their mistakes and keep making the same mistakes over and over again. Once you know why you keep making the same mistakes you can do something about it. Applied information is power and this book is stacked with it.

Thick Face, Black Heart by Chin-Ning Chu

This is one of the best in your face motivational books period. It dismisses the myths about the necessity of positive thinking to be successful. Yes you can be a negative SOB and still lead a very successful life. If you are ever in a place where negotiation is a necessity, you will want to apply the tips from this book. Get it right now. If you do not like this book then you have super high estrogen levels and really need help. This is a testosterone book if there ever was one and any person that wants to take charge of his or her life will love the book.

The Autobiography of Malcolm X by Malcolm X as told to Aldous Huxley

An incredible journey that shows what evolving is all about. Malcolm continued to evolve for the better in his life by continuing challenging his belief systems and his unquenchable desire to grow spiritually. I always find well-written autobiographies interesting as we can learn a great deal from the experiences of others and at the same time learn a lot about ourselves and how to evolve.

The Evolution Of A Cro-magnon by John Joseph

I grew up listening to the legendary band The Cro-Mags. I saw them live many times. Both John Joseph and The Cro-mags bassist Harley Flanagan had a great impact on my life and philosophy. I got into vegetarianism because of them and they showed clearly that one could be strong and fit on a vegetarian diet. John's book was an interesting read for me as it showed how his very difficult life contributed to the music he sang. The origins of The Cro-mags and all the behind things that happened with the band were very entertaining. However, the best part of the book is how John took the immense suffering he went through and found a way to turn it into good for the benefit of other beings. His book encouraged me to take risks with my own book and discuss matters that are very difficult to talk about but are a necessity for all of us. You will find this a great read even if you are not a fan of The Cro-mags.

What Would Machiavelli Do? The Ends Justify The Meanness by Stanley Bing

Several years ago, a friend recommended that I check out a book entitled The Prince by Niccolo Machiavelli. While I thought that the book was excellent; I felt that the language was archaic and that the book was difficult to comprehend. Stanley Bing addressed this problem effectively with his outstanding book. Stanley's book is both entertaining and educational and packed with information that every businessperson needs to know. While I do not necessarily recommend that you practice some of the teachings in Stanley's book, Stanley does go over many things that you absolutely need to know. Knowing when and how people are trying to manipulate you is critical and this book will reveal a great deal about common methods that many people use.

The Art Of War by Sun Tzu

This book is a classic that every man and woman should have in his or her personal library. In fact, if you have not read this book, then get off the computer and go pick up a copy at your local bookstore. If you are too cheap for that, then at least go to your local library and get a copy now. Sun Tzu was a brilliant warrior and you do not have to be a soldier to benefit from his work. Anyone that is a management, a coach, or any other position in which you are in charge of others needs to read this book. This book will teach you how to rally the troops to get the job done. In addition, this book will teach you how to act in various situations to stack the deck in your favor. If that does not motivate you to read it, then you obviously do not care about being successful in any way.

A Book Of Five Rings by Miyamoto Musashi

While this is a book on effective sword fighting, the parallels to self-mastery in any field are amazing. As you learn about how to be an effective swordsman, you will learn how to master whatever your field is. While Sun Tzu's "Art Of War" focuses on how to lead a group, Musashi's "Book Of Five Rings" focuses on how to lead yourself. Both are necessary as being in the world, for most of us it means that we will be interacting with others and need mastery of self to do so effectively.

Unleashing The Warrior Within by Richard Machowicz

I had the pleasure of doing an interview with Richard when I first got started in the training world. Richard is a serious stud and unlike other people that write books about goal setting and motivation, Richard actually practices what he preaches and reveals clearly how his philosophy kept him alive in dozens of near death situations. Richard is a ten-year veteran of the elite Navy Seals and in addition to writing books and doing seminars, Richard provides security for many of Hollywood's elite. He does not insult your intelligence with this book and demonstrates clearly what it takes to be among the elite.

The True Believer: Thoughts On The Nature Of Mass Movements by Eric Hoffer

This is a fascinating analysis of the nature of mass movements and what kind of people are attracted to them. Hoffer covers the conditions that are common that cause people to be drawn to mass movements and the frightening things that people are capable of when they lose their individuality and become part of a group. Hoffer explains that being an individual can be too much of a responsibility for many people to handle and they want the illusory freedom that comes with relinquishing power to another person or group. One of the most interesting quotes from the book is, "They who clamor loudest for freedom are often the ones least likely to be happy in a free society." Many people find more pleasure in being part of a group that is fighting for a cause than being an individual after the goal of the cause has been acquired. If you have ever wanted to know why some people are strong individuals while others seek comfort in the confines of a movement, then this is a book that is for you.

ACHIEVING SUCCESS

Think And Grow Rich by Napoleon Hill

Forget about Tony Robbins and all of the other modern day motivational speakers and self-help gurus. This is the book that started it all and the only one you need to read on how to acquire wealth and achieve your goals. Napoleon engages with the reader effectively and this may very well be the one book that changes your life. I have read it dozens of times and still turn to it when I need extra motivation to carry forward. While the focus of the book is on the acquisition of wealth, you can use the principles that Napoleon reveals to be successful in any endeavor.

Management Secrets of the Rogue Warrior by Richard Marcinko

Richard Marcinko is another veteran of the Navy Seals and knows a thing or two about how to motivate others and what it takes to be successful. What Stanley Bing did for Machiavelli's work, Richard has done for Sun Tzu's work. If you have trouble getting all of the content in "The Art Of War" then read Richard's books to see the teachings in a modern context. Applying Richard's teachings might not make you the most popular person, but it will certainly make you a leader and someone that stands for something, rather than being a politician.

Sex Money Kiss by Gene Simmons

I am not a fan of the band KISS. However, they are one of the most successful rock bands and their success goes way beyond making records. No band has the level of branding that they have. The tremendous success of the band has a great deal to do with Gene Simmons. This is a very interesting book about Gene's philosophy on life and his ideas on how to make a ton of money. Gene is an engaging writer and conveys his points clearly and in an entertaining manner. He is a straight shooter that is not trying to be PC or win the popular vote. You may not agree with everything he believes, but this book will give you a lot to think about.

Pulling Your Own Strings by Dr Wayne Dyer

That is right, the bald guy that is on PBS all of the time talking to a room full of smiling ex-hippies. This is one of Dr. Dyer's older books and is much more hardcore than his new age stuff. Dr. Dyer reveals all of the different ways in which people try to victimize others and the numerous ways in which people victimize themselves. One of the best lines from the book is "Risk taking is at the heart of not being victimized by institutions and bureaucracies." Everyday you will come across people that play power games with you. These people can come in the form of co-workers, friends, family, bosses, etc. Learn how to be aware of people that are trying to pull your strings and what to do to avoid being a victim.

IronMind: Stronger Minds, Stronger Bodies by Randall Strossen, PH.D

Being strong is far more than what you can do physically. If you are strong physically, but weak mentally then you are missing a crucial element of overall strength. The mind plays a great role in the acquisition of physical strength. You are only going to go so far if you are not mentally tough. This book is a compilation of Strossen's excellent monthly columns in Ironman Magazine. If you are interested in enhancing the mental side of strength training, then this is the book for you. After you read the book, you will understand why social pressure can be a growth inhibitor, how inner qualities transfer to outer results, how to develop concentration, and how to forge through frustration.

SPIRITUALITY AND INNER DEVELOPMENT

In today's world it is far too easy to become super materialistic and forget about what is really important in life. I have seen many people grow old and while on their death beds, they often have regrets about not creating enough meaning in their lives. Believe me, you will not wish that you spent more time at the office when your time comes or that you made more money. Life requires balance, and to help you keep yourself and character in tact, you need a strong spiritual foundation. Now, I am not hear to convert anyone to any religion and picking a religion does not necessary mean that you will build a spiritual foundation. That is a path that you have to go alone and discover for yourself. Here are a few books that have helped me with inner development.

The Bhagavad Gita translation by Stephen Mitchell

The Gita is by far my favorite spiritual book. I first read it when I was eighteen and have read it dozens of times over the years. Every time I read it I learn something new. It was the first book that I read that places emphasis the importance of not being attached to the results of our actions and the importance of finding our purpose in life and having the courage to actualize it. The teachings on not being a slave to one's ego and connecting to something much higher than oneself is timeless and very relevant in our world today.

Dune by Frank Herbert

Dune is by far the best science fiction book ever written! The mythology is rich with spiritual teachings and man's struggle for liberation and the inevitability of one's destiny. Much of the politics in the story is relevant to our world today and the parallels are uncanny. The teachings on how to handle fear and persevere are worth the read alone.

Being Peace by Thich Nhat Hanh

Thich Nhat Hanh is a wonderful human being and his books are magical. Thich breaks down the fundamentals of Buddhism into a context that is easy to comprehend and practice. Regardless of what your religious beliefs are, you will find the teachings in this book universal, useful, and insightful.

Way of The Peaceful Warrior by Dan Millman

This is a book that I return to often whenever I want some motivation and clarity in life. It is part fiction and part non-fiction, but all thought provoking and well written. I really like books that use stories to convey spiritual ideas about how to live a deeper life. Through reading about Dan's journey from his mentor "Socrates", you will ponder a great deal on your own life and think about what you can improve on to achieve a higher level of well-being.

The Sufi Path To Mindfulness by Kabir Helminski

The Sufi philosophy contains a wealth of spiritual information. Unfortunately, it can be very difficult to understand many of the concepts. Fortunately, Kabir breaks down the Sufi philosophy into a modern context the masses will have no trouble comprehending. This is a great book that I refer to frequently.

The Celestine Prophecy by James Redfield

James does an amazing job of revealing universal spiritual teachings in an entertaining format. The story is interesting by itself and I think that it is incredible how James skillfully adds in spiritual teachings as you follow the story. I like how he goes over the energy battles that people often have with each other and how destructive they are. Another great book for learning about yourself and others.

Ishmael by Daniel Quinn

There was once a time when man lived with the earth and only took what was necessary. Unfortunately, today people tend to waste the world's resources and the devastating effects on the world and all of the world's beings are only too apparent. Ishmael is a great work of fiction in which a Gorilla tells an unlikely hero about what course needs to be taken to save the world. This is a very entertaining and creative book with a timely message.

EDITING CREDITS

Sarina Derksen for final editing And proofreading for all chapters

TERESA BLAZEY EDITED THE FOLLOWING CHAPTERS

- Is Having A Positive Attitude Overrated?
- The Dangers Of Always Accommodating
- Don't Rely On Your Illusory Memory
- Networking Myths! It Is More Than Who You Know
- Don't Ever Get Involved With Network Marketing Companies
- Why Your Need For Praise Is Holding You Back
- Are We Becoming A Nation Of Orthorexics?
- Are You Prepared To Actually Take Advice?
- Doing What You Love Is Hard Work
- Your Flawed Decision Making Process Is Why You Fail
- Addiction To Constant Entertainment Makes Success Impossible
- Are You A Research Addict Or An Action Addict?
- We Are Great At Kidding Ourselves
- The High Price Of Ownership
- Eleven Reasons Why We Make Mistakes And Why We Keep Making Them
- Fear Is The Ultimate Manipulation Method
- Are You Capable Of Evil? Yes You Are
- Use Pressure To Be Successful
- Jealousy Is A Wasted Emotion
- Being Risk Adverse Makes You Success Adverse

- Will You Let A "Knife" Prevent You From Conquering Your Goal?
- Is Experience Overrated?
- I Never Saved Anything for the Swim Back
- Waiting For Permission Is A Sure Fire Way To Fail
- The Timing Is Never Perfect
- Is Happiness Determined By Our Genetics?
- Is Happiness Determined By Our Genetics? Part Two
- Stop Complaining And Take Charge Of Your Life

ALEX GOETZFRIED EDITED THE FOLLOWING CHAPTERS

- It Is Time To Live Life Aggressively
- The Necessity Of Negative Thinking
- Being Attached To Results Is Holding You Back
- Why You Must Optimize Your Hormones
  Do You Have The Courage To Evolve?
- The Real Battle Is Within
- Embrace Compassion Fully Or Be Destroyed By Anger
- Being A Great Teacher Is Not Easy
- What Are You Prepared To Do Now?

ABOUT THE AUTHOR

Mike Mahler is a fitness information provider based in Las Vegas, NV. Mike has been a strength trainer and kettlebell instructor for over nine years and has taught workshops all over the US and overseas. His current focus is on the field of hormone optimization via nutrition, training, and lifestyle.

Mike is also a respected writer, known for his honest and fluff-free style, and has written over a hundred articles for publications such as: *Muscle & Fitness, Men's Fitness, Hardcore Muscle Magazine, Planet Muscle, Testosterone Magazine, Ironman Magazine, Ironman Magazine Japan, Industry Magazine,* and *Exercise Magazine For Men.* Mike has also been featured in *Muscle & Fitness, UPN News,* and *CBS News.*

For more info, go to www.mikemahler.com